Why didn't I 'THINK' of that?

The creative power of Ideas at Work!

BOB 'IDEA MAN' HOOEY

Author, *Legacy of Leadership*

6th edition (updated for 2014)

Foreword

"There is no doubt that creativity is the most important human resource of all. Without creativity, there would be no progress, and we would be forever repeating the same patterns." **Edward de Bono**

From a very young age, whether doodling with crayons or solving riddles, I've relentlessly pursued my passion for creativity. Early in my professional life, I started a career in advertising which gave me the perfect opportunity to bring ideas to life and turn my passion into an idea mill which put bread on my table.

Creativity is the engine that propels the idea mill; the very substance which can transform reality from boring to utterly exciting. It allows us to envision a different outcome and imagine exponential possibilities. But beyond ideas, changing the future to shape it to our vision requires strong leadership and perseverance to implement them.

"Over the years, it became clear to me that acting upon an idea was by far more challenging than coming up with the idea itself."
Nabil Doss 2014

So, I've grown to deeply appreciate and respect the combined power of ideas and leadership. Great ideas, at least the ones that really stick over time and make a difference, are usually brought forth by visionary and generous leaders.

Ideas... Leadership... Generosity of Spirit

That pretty much describes my good friend Bob Hooey. In fact, I'd be hard pressed to pick one word over the other to depict Bob. He embodies an interesting blend of these three qualities and, somehow, consistently manages to leave his unique watermark on everything he undertakes.

Known as the *Idea Man*, Bob has actively contributed to the growth of the Canadian Association of Professional Speakers (CAPS). Through his leadership and personal involvement, he was instrumental in helping our CAPS Foundation to take off at a critical time.

He was bestowed with the much coveted *Spirit of CAPS* Award for his generosity of spirit, his constant positive outlook, and for being a great inspiration to his peers.

I will always remember his words, a few years ago in Halifax, at our CAPS National convention. As I stepped off the stage after a first showcase speech in front of my speaker colleagues, he tapped me on the shoulder and gave me a heartfelt and very strategic compliment. He simply said *"What you've done in 5 minutes, many of us wouldn't be able to do in an hour."*

In one sentence he had focused on the essence of what my brand would eventually be and made me feel like a hero. He truly acted as a leader, in his own generous way.

When, many moons ago, Bob was a kitchen designer he consistently came up with fresh creative solutions for his clients. Now, still in his own generous way, Bob poured all of his experience, his savoir faire, and his expertise into this inspiring book full of practical ideas, for us to enjoy and apply. It's the blueprint for a new idea space; an amazing recipe book and, above all, great food for thought!

With such an abundance of ideas at our fingertips, we really have no more reason to say **"Why didn't I THINK of that!"**

Nabil Doss
Expert in Influential Communication
2013 President, Canadian Association of Professional Speakers
www.nabildoss.com

Editor's note: I also remember telling Nabil, a short time after he was elected to our CAPS National board, that I thought he would make a great president. Guess his fellow board members agreed as he was picked to move up to that role in later years. He was! He served us with distinction and dedication last year and my respect and admiration for my amazingly talented and creative friend has grown.

3

Preface

A wise man once told me, **"*My ability to earn would be directly dependent on my ability to 'creatively' solve client problems and to help people make better decisions.*"** I've taken his words to heart and worked diligently to make what I provide connect in my writing and client engagements!

As committed business owners and professionals, we are paid for our ability to creatively solve our client's problems by the providing services or products. As innovative leaders, managers, owners, sales professionals, or even association executives, 'creativity' and/or innovation is our stock-in-trade as we serve and solve our numerous client and membership needs.

The tools, tips, and techniques shared in *'Why Didn't I THINK of That?'* can be **applied** in at least **three directions:**

- Problem-solving and decision making
- Strategic planning for business and career enhancement
- Tapping your inner genius or Creative S.O.U.L.

It has been my experience that the 'tools', tips, tid-bits, and techniques in this book will help you in the process of defining the direction and outlining the creative process you need to 'successfully' reach the goals you set for yourself and your respective teams.

These creativity tools are 'essential' in helping you birth your dreams or in solving perplexing problems for your clients/customers and/or members you encounter. They can better help you form, train, and lead your teams.

The title *'Why Didn't I THINK of That?'* came from remarks often heard from design clients upon presentation of their 'new' kitchen. We've rewritten this 6th edition (2014) with a focus to help fellow leaders blend creativity into their leadership styles; and to assist business owners and managers blend creativity into better attracting and serving their prospective clients and leading their teams. Enjoy!

Bob 'Idea Man' Hooey
Creative catalyst and author

Copyright and Credits

Why Didn't I THINK of That? 6th edition (Updated for 2014)
The creative power of Ideas at Work!

By **Bob 'Idea Man' Hooey**, Accredited Speaker, 2011 Spirit of CAPS recipient. Prolific author of 30 plus business, leadership, sales, and career success publications

This book by **Bob 'Idea Man' Hooey** was originally published in 1999 and has been updated numerous times over the years. This 6th edition was rewritten for re-release in 2014.

Cover design: **David Saxby**, www.SparkCommunications.com
Photos of Bob: **Dov Friedman**, www.photographybyDov.com
Editorial, layout and design: **Irene Gaudet**, Vitrak Creative Services, www.VitrakCreative.com

ISBN 13: 978-1499113303 ISBN 10: 1499113307

Printed in the United States 10 9 8 7 6 5 4 3 2 1

Success Publications
Legacy of Leadership series
Box 10, Egremont, AB T0A 0Z0
www.successpublications.ca
Creative office: 1-780-736-0009

Table of Contents

Why Didn't I THINK of That?
The creative power of Ideas at Work!

As we begin...

"Leadership," says Peter Drucker *"is lifting a person's vision to higher sights, raising a person's performance to a higher standard, and building a personality beyond its normal limitations." Now that is <u>creative</u> vision!*

The foundations of effective, personal leadership whether in a business, a career, or leading a volunteer group, start with 'each' person actively taking responsibility for their own actions as part of a group. Personal leadership precedes powerful, effective leadership in any role. Those foundations are enhanced in feeling confident enough to suggest, create ideas, and accept revisions in team goals and performance.

You might be asking, *"What does leadership have to do with* **creativity and innovation?"** Quite frankly, everything! If we are to successfully learn new styles of applied problem-solving, unlock our creativity, and increase our ability to make better decisions, more creative decisions; we must be willing to take personal leadership in using them in our own activities and in the interaction with our fellow workers, team members, and clients.

"Our productivity - often survival - does not depend solely on how much effort we expend, but on whether or not the effort we invest is in the right direction." We must create visionary, innovative road maps that will guide us and our colleagues to greater success.

Peter Drucker also said, *"Management is doing things right; Leadership is doing the right things."* That means **creating better options to precede our decisions and their implementation**. Our goal in effectively handling major problems, challenges, and mistakes is to being able to cut through to the root causes and then creatively develop real innovative solutions to put into action.

My objective is to assist you in acquiring some new problem solving models and introducing a few creativity nudges and tools that will help you in your personal life, career, and interaction with your clients and co-workers. We will work through the problem solving process to creatively outline creative solutions - workable solutions that can be implemented today!

I hope to help you discover a new creative approach and mindset to the problems you may encounter. I challenge you to see them as creative opportunities to grow and change the way you live and/or do business.

Some objectives for enhancing our creativity might be:

- More accurate information - increased productivity by better communication and application of creativity in the workplace.

- Effective coordination of activities - how do I fit in the big picture? Improving the flow of ideas - both internally (up and down) and externally.

- Facilitating the decision making process - being a creative agent of change.

- Training – cross-training, uniform training, and to provide an interactive forum (time permitting).

- Building morale - encouraging teamwork and mutual support.

Occasionally, we need to 'pause' to gain a higher perspective to make sure we are still heading in the right direction. Our efficiency can be misdirected if we are not going where we want in pursuit of our goals.

In a previous life, I worked as a kitchen designer solving challenges and creating amazing home improvement projects for my clients. I remember driving home to Calgary from Lethbridge, AB early one winter morning. I had been working with Southern Alberta clients all week and wanted to get back into the office early so I could drop off my paperwork, get a bit of catch up done, and start my weekend. I was making good time cruising down the highway with the radio playing some great tunes. Then, I noticed a sign saying Castelgar, BC only 65 miles. Whoa! I pulled over and collected my thoughts. How could that be? I was heading home to Calgary, Alberta! Somehow in my overworked, tired brain I had driven right through Fort Macleod and missed at least two BIG highway signs reminding me to turn 'right', to head 'north' to Calgary. Sure I was making great time, but I was going in the 'wrong' direction.

One of the biggest lessons I've learned about creative problem solving is: **There is always a solution.** Often, there are **a multitude of solutions.** If your problem is industry specific, you might want to talk to others in your industry and **'Thunder-think'** or brainstorm some answers. Or you might want to bring it to your next Chamber of Commerce, networking, mastermind, or association meeting.

The other lesson learned: **I'm not the 'only' one with a problem. Sharing a problem can lead to solving it.** Someone not directly involved in your problem may see a solution or thread that unravels it, because of the difference in his or her perspective or experience or because they are not emotionally involved!

I remember a story of an elevator being built at the El Cortez hotel in San Diego, CA. Seems the owner and architect were discussing timing needed to remodel and add another internal one and how long the hotel would be shut down. A janitor over heard and, worried about his job, asked what was happening and why? The architect hautly asked if he had a better idea. He suggested building it on the outside – the first of its kind in the world. Hmm!

We've re-written this 'work-in-progress' (*a form of innovation*) specifically to guide you and provide tips, techniques, and creative problem-solving models that work in the real world. We've included tips to help you set 'strategies for success' and make effective decisions for your career and organization. We've created this 6th edition to share new ideas and stories to help in your journey.

I believe passionately in the information presented and enjoy the opportunity to pass it on to you.

I want you to 'succeed' and will do what's needed to facilitate that process. I want to see you use this information in your dealings with each other and in better serving the needs of your clients. In my longer training programs I coach, confront, and confirm as necessary to keep my audience member's creativity flowing and keep us on track during our time together.

I'd love the opportunity to share a few ideas in person with you and your respective teams

Bob 'Idea Man' Hooey, CKD-Emeritus, Accredited Speaker, 2011 Spirit of CAPS recipient

email me: bob@ideaman.net

"Change comes with such rapidity that businesses must anticipate tomorrow's needs today, because the distinction between today and tomorrow is increasingly blurred. Innovation is the way of life, central to how an organization conducts itself, becomes fundamental to corporate survival."
Nicholas Imparato *and* **Oren Harrari**, *from 'Jumping the Curve'*

CREATIVITY

" Creativity has been built into everyone of us;
it's part of our design.

Each of us lives less of the life God intended
for us when we choose not to live out
the creative powers we possess. "
Ted Engstrom

"Creativity is especially expressed in the ability to
make connections, to make associations, to turn
things around and express them in a new way."
Tim Hansen

"One of the major factors which differentiates creative
people from lesser creative people is that creative
people pay attention to their small ideas."
Roger von Oech

"We do not yet trust the unknown powers of thought."
Ralph Waldo Emerson

"Nothing is more dangerous than an idea,
when it's the only idea you have."
Linus Pauling

Creativity is a survival tool instilled at birth. However, it is a tool that needs to be 'enhanced,' 'honed,' and 'sharpened' as we move forward into life; more so as we enhance our career skills and roles as creative leaders, business owners, and top level professionals. This book gives you creative tools to do just that.

How to get the 'best' use from your copy of
Why Didn't I THINK of That?

'Why Didn't I THINK of That?' contains a wide range of creative tips, techniques, stories, examples, and innovative ideas. Our aim is to help you improve the way you 'train' and lead your team for shared growth and profitable long-term success working with your clients to creatively solve their needs. It evolved into its present format (from a college level program) with the inclusion of stories, ideas, and first-hand experience based on conversations, copious notes, and first-hand observations of productive fellow leaders and innovative retailers. It was made personal from experiences leading and being on a variety of teams across North America and the globe. It is seasoned with my own creative business tips and experiences in retail, direct sales, and professional services.

It has been updated with a creative focus to assist professionals, owners, and leaders more profitably enhance their business with innovative customer engagement. It is designed as a creativity guide for those who want to take personal leadership providing a purpose and making a positive contribution in the lives of their teams and in interactions with their clients.

This is <u>not</u> just a book for casual reading. It is a book to be *chewed*, to be *dipped* into, and *leveraged* as a resource or reference guide. It is a workbook with provocative questions that help you decide what you want to accomplish with your life, your leadership, and with your client and team relationships. It is your creativity resource, so mark it, highlight it, and make notes in the margins.

To get the best from this book, first visit the Table of Contents to identify which chapters and/or topics meet your most critical, time sensitive needs. Read them carefully and make sure you understand the guidelines and advice given. Some of the topics may not be of direct interest to you (now), depending on your needs. You may wish to read some of the other chapters so that you can understand the needs of other leaders, 'client', or customer service scenarios.

'Why Didn't I THINK of That?' does not contain ALL the answers. It contains a collection of thoughts, notes, clippings, tips, techniques, lessons learned, and ideas shared primarily from one learner, one business leader's (one retailer's) viewpoint, mine. It is simply intended as an aid to your reflection, learning, and inspiration – a resource that you can draw upon. We trust it will help you develop and build both your confidence and profitable competence as a more creative leader, manager, and business owner.

A more productive approach would be to take the tips and concepts presented here and blend them with your own leadership style, personality, and creativity. Keep in mind your own time constraints and 'comfort zone' as a leader, business manager, or professional. Generate unique and perhaps personalized ideas on how you can create, give, and improve your interaction and action with your teams.

'Why Didn't I THINK of That?' – **6th edition** is designed to offer you flexibility in how you leverage it for your personal and professional use.

1) You can easily sit down for an hour or two and read it **cover-to-cover**. This is a great way to start by getting a feel for what is included, especially for newer or emerging leaders, managers, or owners (those who want to take more personal leadership for their lives and better equip their teams to grow) who want to gain the full benefit from their investment.

A word of advice: *'Why Didn't I THINK of That?'* is the result of 29 plus years of personal study, first-hand experience, and observation in a variety of leadership, retail, business, and sales roles; as well as support and coaching roles for executive clients and their respective teams. It might seem overwhelming or confusing at first with the range of information included. Once you have done a quick read of the whole book, identify particular sections or tips that interest you and work on manageable chunks.

2) You can select one chapter or section and work to incorporate the ideas you discover into your own specific leadership role, client engagement, or business building situation.

3) You can look at the Table of Contents and jump straight to the tips or areas of study that particularly interest you.

We have attempted to incorporate something of benefit for everyone, regardless of your current career level or skill in business or leadership. You might even find some contradictory advice in different parts of the book! ☺ This is because there is no single, universal 'right answer' – you must find what is a right fit for you, your objective, and/or your team's specific needs. What works for you is what is best! Choose it, try it, and adapt it as needed to serve you in your quest to be a more effective business person and impactful leader. Take control of how you allocate, invest, or leverage your time and interaction with your staff and clients.

We've written it to help you guide your teams to become more creative, productive, and profitably enhance your business dealings with your clients.

The Six Creative Indicators

Can you tell who is more likely to be a creative addition to your team? Can you separate the 'really' creative from the herd? Well according to research there are six basic indicators that might help in your quest to attract creative people for your team. People who rank high or exhibit more of these characteristics tend to be more creative.

Idea volume and fluency

This is an area where volume 'actually' counts. It may take 30 average ideas to yield one great one. Creative people tend to be better at generating ideas, even if most of them have little long term or applicable commercial value. Our minds are very much like a 'muscle' in that we tend to work better when we warm them up. They work better when they are exercised on a regular basis too. Our best ideas often come after we have worked through the more basic ones.

Slow to jump to conclusions or judge

You tend to get more high quality ideas when judgment is withheld. This is the secret to effective brainstorming or 'Thunder-thinking'. Judging cuts off the creative flow of ideas. Judging tends to look for what doesn't fit or won't work verses exploring possibilities and potential. Creativity is willing to explore the options and potentials.

Imagination and flexibility

Creativity in its essence is based on flexible thinking. Creative people tend to exhibit almost a kid-like curiosity about life. Acting as if the world can be as you imagine it enhances your creativity. *"The best way to predict the future is to create or invent it."*

Concentration and focus

Both of these traits are 'critical aspects' of creativity. Concentration is staying focused on a particular subject, even when you are tired, bored or frustrated. Creative behaviors are able to ignore or tune out distractions and outside stimuli while working to solve a problem or reach a goal.

Able to deal with ambiguity

Creativity is dealing with the vague and unformed to create the clear and concise. Creative people tend to be able to handle ambiguity where there is no clearly defined right or wrong. Creative people have a willingness to see all sides of a situation and to remain in questioning mode rather than rushing to find the answer. They keep going past the 'first' right answer to explore for the 'best' answer or innovative solution.

Able to handle disorder

Creative people tend to handle or even prefer disorder. Forget the stereotype of the absent minded professor with stacks all around the office. This may be valid, but **disorder is not necessarily 'mess'**. Disorder refers to non-linear thinking, shaking up the normal order, status quo, or non-symmetrical design.

Keep these six indicators in mind when you are looking to recruit a member of your Mastermind Alliance, sales and marketing team, or support team. People do exhibit their creative traits if you are willing to look and analyze their behaviour. Remember we can unleash our creativity, too. *I have sprinkled brain boosters and creative ideas for your fun throughout this book! Stop and play with them!*

Ideas that are weird – perhaps?

Innovation and idea generation are, at the very basics, about being curious and courageous; curious about life, courageous about challenging the status quo, and then making changes to make it better.

This is where those who lead creatively excel. They are not afraid to go outside the confines of their narrow field and to borrow, beg, and sometimes 'steal' ideas from other fields and industries. **Great ideas are transferable!** It is a good management practice to look at your 'norms' and ask yourself the 'contrarian' or flip side of the equation questions. This is where innovation and the real creative spark exist. That doesn't mean you always throw away what you are currently using. At times it is still very effective and may be the most productive use of your time, resources, and energy. **What if there is a better way, a more productive way, a more cost effective way, and your competitor finds it first?** Hmm?

The secret to thriving in our competitive, and by now everyone understands globally competitive market, is being constantly on the 'improve' and sometimes that means 'improve' to find the answers to the questions your existing and potential clients are asking. So keep questioning and keep on the quest to tap into your creative genius!

How to Handle the Idea Killers in Your Life!

YOU have this great dream or this fantastic idea bursts into your head. You're excited about the unlimited possibilities and can't wait to share it with your co-workers, closest friends, and, of course, your family.

What is their reaction? All too often, their initial reaction is to ridicule the idea, to point out its flaws, to remind you about your lack of education, your lack of money, your lack of experience, or to point out how so and so tried it and it didn't work. Whew! The result ... too often, you stop and let your dreams die, be minimized, or give up on your ideas. You've let your colleagues, friends, and family opinions and criticism 'rob' you of your future and your solid potential for greatness!

Why do they do that? Well it might be for a variety of reasons, some of them with the best intentions. It might simply be their concern to see you avoid getting hurt or to side step what they see as a path to failure.

It may be, and often is, based on their 'own fears' projected onto your action and life. It might be due to a personal failure on their part and a fear that, if you succeed, they will lose you. Or a fear they will have to deal with the reality that, just maybe, they could have done something about their 'seemingly impossible' situation. Your potential for success scares them or makes them a bit nervous about their own chances, neglect, or inactivity.

How do we handle these 'helpers' or **'idea killers'** in our life? One of the best ways is to be aware of their existence and seek to avoid them in areas of vulnerability. I don't mean to cut them off completely. Just realize that they are not committed to or understanding of your dreams and desires. Be kind, as they do not know that they don't get it. Don't waste your energy on them.

Make a conscious choice to keep these areas private, especially during the embryonic or incubation stages of establishing your goals, dreams, or ideas. Maintain your focus and keep moving forward to see your idea or dream become a reality.

As someone once wrote, **"Show no regrets for the past, no fear for the future. Expect to win – expect GREATNESS!"**

It's a funny thing in life, if you refuse to accept anything but the best, you often get it! We may not get to choose our family, but we do have full control over our friends and over the amount of time we spend with colleagues, friends, and family. This is where we make the decisions and connections that help shape or determine our destiny.

In life, there are those who would kill our dreams and those who would, if asked, help nurture our dreams. We can identify and choose each group in which to associate and productively invest our time. Find your champions!

One of the most effective ways of dealing with an idea killer is by **doing your homework.** If you have researched your dream and have done your due diligence, some can even be brought around to being 'at least' a neutral observer. And, when you succeed, watch them come out then!

Use feedback from these idea killers as mirrors that may show you your 'blind spots'. Often, they see things that you might miss in the heat of passion. Keep in mind their input is for **information 'only'** and check it for relevance and accuracy before you allow it to impact or influence your decisions.

Demonstrate by your strategic actions that you're committed to seeing 'this' project through to completion. Often our past track record of starting and not completing projects may influence their support and enthusiasm. This is especially true with immediate family members.

Idea killers may occasionally become allies, but it takes massive work on your part to win them over to your team. Keep focused on your Goals and Dreams! Don't let another person's critical attitude determine your worth or your future. Don't let them stop you! You don't know how high you can fly until you spread your wings and take to the sky. Please don't let another person's limiting beliefs, no matter how well-intentioned, stop you attempting to dream big, to compete for the ultimate prize, achieving your personal or professional dream. Create the future you imagine!

It is too easy for those around you, who are hopelessly mired in their own mediocrity, to criticize you for trying to follow your dream or acting to implement your great idea.

"A rock pile ceases to be a rock pile the moment a single man contemplates it, bearing within him the image of a cathedral."

Antoine de Saint-Exupery – The Little Prince

'Creating Time' as a part of your
Why Didn't I THINK of That? journey

Our *'Creating Time to Sell, Lead, or Manage'* program was originally created and delivered for the BC Management Team of the **St. John Ambulance**, with all of their branch managers coming together. The objective for our session was a skillful blending of solid sales, business building, and service principles with a good use of time to allow their respective teams to be more productive in their customer service efforts. It was very well received. We've spent time over the past dozen years refocusing and expanding it as a tool to offer our clients to help them succeed in attracting, profitably selling, and retaining customers, plus building referral and repeat business.

The secrets and tools we cover in our on-site workshops have allowed top performing professionals, their managers, and their staff to find creative ways to be more pro-active in 'reaching' and 'retaining' clients for their organizations. We include this brief excerpt for your reference and use.

While flying to a speaking engagement in the US, I read a study that indicated the **average sales person puts in a 53-hour week and this might be a low estimate.** *Yet, in spite of this long week,* **less than 8 hours of face-to-face sales activity was recorded (about 15%).** *More recently, I read that the average business owner, leader, or executive has 40-60 hours of unfinished business on their agenda at any one time. Sound familiar? Whew!*

Something is radically wrong with this picture. **Work more and produce less** is not a good indicator for any organization that wants to survive or thrive in an extremely hectic and competitive market. Whatever happened to 'work smarter not harder'? We are too busy, overwhelmed, and distracted; and that impacts our ability to serve and sell to our clients. We are too busy to invest the necessary time in training our staff in their efforts to be creatively equipped to succeed. We are too busy to truly enhance our business and generate all the sales potentially available. Sad, really!

To be effective in business in general, we've been telling our audiences and clients that we must deal creatively with **three areas as they relate to our potential clients.**

- **Pain**
- **Gain**
- **Sustaining**

The degree that you creatively work 'with' your clients/customers to take care of these three areas, will impact your profitability and long-term viability. Each area has its 'specific focus' and profit center. In the sales process each area has its impact and effectiveness. At times we work with clients/customers who have one or more of these areas as their focus. The time we spend finding out what their 'real' need is, increases the likelihood that we will be the one engaged to help solve it.

If we only help people with their **'pain'** - will they 'still' need us when it is gone? What motivation do people have to visit a doctor or dentist when they are feeling well? A word to the wise! Helping them **'gain'** offers a bit more opportunity to serve and build a profitable long-term business relationship built on repeat purchases and referrals.

If you can work with them through their **'pain'**, help them **'gain'** in the process; and then take them through to help them grow and **'sustain growth'** you can become a major, vital part of their team (business or life) for years to come. That is taking full advantage of leveraging your time in the customer service/sales process for maximum return.

They will deal with you time and again, if you help them 'see' and receive the value you provide. I offer it as a mental jog to focus on using your time more creatively and to wisely blend proven sale principles (perhaps you've had a sales course) into the mix. Having said that, how can you focus on the above three success focused tools; if you are bogged down with minutia and paperwork or are unwisely using your time each day in non-productive, non-sales oriented activities?

Ask yourself; no, make a decision to track and analyze exactly how much time you 'actually' spend in the creative sales/customer service process. The results will surprise you and they may even scare you! Many of us in the sales /customer service field find ourselves easily side tracked. We spend time doing 'paper work', filling out reports, or 'busy work'; chatting on the phone, chatting with our colleagues, reading the paper, taking long breaks, and other such 'non-productive' activities.

Am I saying to eliminate these in their entirety? NO! Simply be aware of where you invest your time – and track the results to ensure that your investment is well placed. You **'make money'** in business primarily when you are in face-to-face or phone-to-phone sales or follow up contact with your clients. You **'earn that money'** by delivering on what you contract and you **'leverage that money'** by good client contact and ongoing service. But first, you need to be and/or keep in contact with them.

Prospecting is both a creative and productive use of time in the sales/customer service process – how much time do you spend doing it? Have you developed a systematic way to track and follow up on each one?

Have you set-aside specific times each day to contact potential clients? When? Have you set aside specific times to maintain contact with existing clients to find out when and where you can help them again?

Repeat sales are the best and the most profitable ones! *I love it when a client I've spoken for calls and asks me to come again. Referrals don't hurt the process either! Many of my clients hear about me from another client, speaker, or trainer and then call to see if I can help their teams. Perhaps I can help you and your team?*

Have you set aside specific time for follow up, to make sure your current clients received what you promised and are satisfied with their relationship with you?

According to **Marketing Metrics** your probability of selling to existing clients/customers is 60-70% whereas your probability with new prospects is only 5-20%. According to the **White House Office of Consumer Affairs** loyal customers are worth up to 10 times as much as their initial purchase. Factor in, acquiring new clients is 6-7 times more expensive than keeping existing ones and you'll start seeing the value of investing in and maintaining good customer service.

Creativity in leveraging service is a success tool for the top performing professional, business owner, and champion sales person. It amazes them when you call back – so few sales people do! It helps convert them into your champions and fans when you follow-up and ensure they are happy. When you find out early when something is not working correctly or needs adjustment, fix it and go the extra mile to make them happy!

Have you worked to make it easier for your clients to find you, get the information they need, and track their order or service process? UPS and FEDEX use on-line tracking systems as very effective sales and marketing tools. **Michael Hammer** drives home the point about being **ETDBW** (easy to do business with) in *'The Agenda'*. Add it to your sales library! How easy are you to do business with? Create connections with your clients!

We continually evolve our primary website **www.ideaman.net** by expanding and enhancing its different customer driven segments For example, we've created on-line resources and downloadable articles.

My web-based work is becoming a series of true value-added client-centric sites, as well as very productive and profitable. It is time well spent in creating time to sell, lead, or manage my business and customer contact relationships. For example: www.SecretSellingTips.com

Have you 'systemized' your work area and computers to make it easier for you or your colleagues to access information, client files, literature, etc to better and more quickly serve your clients?

Have you spent specific time 'thinking' about all the potential challenges or questions that might come up from a prospective client? Have you discussed these challenges and the productive solutions you and your organization provide? Are your staff fully informed and well 'trained' in helping clients with their challenges? Do you have solid, well-researched, value-enhancing, creative answers ready and burned into your mind? Why not?

If you invest even a small amount of time working on these questions and implementing the results of your deliberations – you'll find yourself able to spend more time on the sales, service, and marketing process. You'll also find you will attract more clients, receive better quality referrals, and garner more profitable repeat business.

Amazingly enough when you are '*Creating Time to Sell, Lead, or Manage*', as a part of your business and career focus - you end up selling and making more money too! Even if you are not directly in sales, you may be able to apply these creative tips and technique in helping your colleagues, members, and community creatively move ahead.

Brain boosters: (take a minute and let your brain play with one or two) Warming up your brain to engage your creative genius works!

Finish this sentence 20 times: People are most generous when _____

Design the cover for a new book called, 'The best things in life are creative'

Think of your childhood songs. Sing one to someone else today.

What if birds barked and dogs chirped? What would that be like?

Write a letter to yourself telling you why you are creative. Be specific!

Create 5 new brand names for a line of ladies watches. Men's watches.

Check out '*Running TOO Fast? Create time to lead and still have a life!*' (Updated for 2014) *www.SuccessPublications.ca*

Change is a creative choice

In life, we often have the 'opportunity' thrust upon us to make changes. A death, a major illness, **or a major economic upheaval** can force us to take stock of our lives at that point and sometimes make radical changes. For example, 9-11 and the 2007-08 economic melt-down did that for many of us.

In our rapidly changing economy, we find businesses and professional associations being stretched and tested as competition becomes increasingly global. Staffing has become more challenging and so has training and marketing. Clients are becoming more demanding and specific in what they want. Time and resources are constantly being stretched.

Change is pushed on us everywhere we turn. We can't avoid change, can we? That's what too many business owners think and miss their full potential. Even some of the most creative companies can lag behind if they don't continue their path of ongoing innovation and product or service creation.

But isn't it better to seize the opportunities to change and grow? Isn't it better to be someone who is open to learn, stretch, and push yourself past your comfort zone? Move into your winner's zone!

This change is a creative choice! Life is a series of changes and choices. Why not control their direction and pace!

"Searching for the peak performer within yourself has one basic meaning - You recognize yourself as a person who was born, not as a peak performer but as a learner. With the capacity to grow, change, and reach for the highest possibilities of human nature, you regard yourself as a person in process. Not perfect, but a person who keeps asking: What more can I be? What else can I achieve that will benefit me and my company? What will contribute to my family and my community?" Charles Garfield

Ask yourself these questions. Allow your honest reactions to reflect the changes in your attitudes and actions that may need to be addressed to maximize your life and dealings.

- What do I really want to accomplish in my life? What is my biggest dream or goal?
- What would I like my company to accomplish? Where do I want my career to go?
- What am I afraid of? What is stopping me? What keeps me up at night?

- What do I need to change to make it work? When do I need to change it?
- When will I commit to start making these changes?

Will you have the courage to change? Will you commit to being your best and to creatively build your business or association to maximize its potential?

Remember the words of wisdom from retailer J.C. Penny: **"No one need live a minute longer as he/she is, because the creator endowed us with the ability to change ourselves."**

Answering these questions will have given you a 'glimpse' of what needs to be changed to make your dreams and goals a reality. The secret is in putting foundations under your dreams and actions to your goals. The secret to **unlocking your 'creativity' potential** is accessing your ability to embrace and use change for mutual benefit. **The choice is yours!**

Business observations on applied creativity

When teaching this program in person I often pull examples from business to illustrate creative techniques. Many of these you know, but they still ring true.

For example, **Barbie** is a creative example of a product with a built in add-on or up-sell capacity. She comes with one outfit and you are encouraged to buy more and to accessorize her life. You can even buy her friends too. Interesting!

Domino's built a profitable slice of the pizza business by simply promising to get it there hot and ready to eat. This differentiated them from those cold and greasy competitors. What can you do to differentiate yourself from your competition? What can you create as your unique selling proposition?

Telus, AT&T, and the satellite or cable outlets taught how to take a basic service and bundle items clients want for a higher rate. What can you bundle?

Starbucks took an espresso machine previously seen in Italian and European coffee shops and built and empire around the world selling their 'experience'.

Canadian trapper, **Charles Birdseye** observed that the fish he caught during the winter froze quickly. When he cooked them they still tasted fresh. This observant concept was the start of the frozen food industry.

Federal Express applied an idea (central hub) used by banks in clearing checks and documents as the basis for an effective and efficient delivery system.

One percent better!

"Excellence results from doing 100 things 1 percent better, rather than one thing 100 percent better." Author Unknown

One of the biggest obstacles to growth is the 'misguided' quest for the big idea, the big break, the big sale, or the big change. In reality, success, sales, and growth happen one step at a time, one improvement at a time, and often a simple, one-percent-at-a-time.

Sure there are many stories of major breakthroughs and advances; perhaps you've even experienced one or more yourself. However, when you look at what led up to them, you'll often see multiple efforts to improve, research, prepare, and experiment. This is often the case in my life and business as I work and prepare in advance of the successful completion or creative breakthrough.

It would be so easy, if we could simply wait until the big million dollar idea drops into our brains or laps and then reap the benefits. It would also be unrealistic to live that way. It would be like buying a lotto ticket as a means of paying your monthly bills. Top performers and leaders are never fully satisfied with where they or their teams are. They have what many would call 'creative discontent' in that they can always see ways of tweaking or making it better. Many of the ones I meet or work with live this way.

Peters and Waterman (*In Search of Excellence*) wrote, *"The essence of excellence is the thousand concrete, minute-to-minute actions performed by everyone in an organization to keep a company on its course."*

Sam Walton of Wal-Mart fame was famous for looking at his competition with the eye of learning 'one thing' he could use to make what he and his team did a bit better. He built a large, successful, multi-national company from a very little one by applying this concept of continuous improvement.

Jack Welsh made some amazing and profitable changes in GE by doing the same thing. **What are your competitors doing better that you can apply?**

Are there 10 to 15 areas where you can make changes that will give you a 1% improvement?

Write the ideas for improvement down and schedule specific time to make them happen.

One percent better can be your rallying call in the pursuit of excellence and success in your leadership, career, or company. Create and then change!

A lesson from the Wizzard of Menlo Park

Many people think of **Thomas Edison** as being a pinnacle of originality and invention. That is still true! However, did you know he was also very open to borrowing or leveraging from concepts originated by others? For example, he saw how bottle caps worked and applied that concept to creating the screw in light bulb. Hmm?

We may not all aspire to be an Edison, but we can certainly learn to approach generating or applying ideas like he did. We don't have to pull ideas out of our proverbial hats on demand. We can use our research and 'applied' curiosity to propel us to greater creativity in dealing with the tasks at hand. Often, the idea we need, the spark of inspiration, might be contained in the ideas or brains of another 'genius'. Reach out and learn from other creative people around you.

Why not start a creativity collection of brain starters: articles and pictures from a diverse range of resources, toys, tools, and other interesting objects. Look for influences from a diverse well of wisdom and wonder. When you are faced with a challenge where you want to bring your creative muscle (brain) to bear, bring it out and play for awhile.

Play mental pin ball and make connections to kick start your creativity; then dig in and create! Use the brain boosters we include here as a mental warm up or kick start for your brain. Why not use them as mental warm ups with your team to kick start regular brainstorming sessions?

"Around here, however, we don't look backwards for very long. We keep moving forward, opening up new doors and doing new things, because we're curious... and curiosity keeps leading us down new paths." Walt Disney Company

What if?

A few questions to ponder...

What if you could have anything you wanted in life? **What if** you had all the talent, skills, money, and help you needed to accomplish your wildest dreams? **What if** you could find the solution to the challenge you face? **What if** you were really in charge of your life? What would you do? Where would you go? Who would you become? Hmm!

Often, we encounter people mired in the day-to-day reality who have forgotten how to dream. People who have had their dreams 'down-sized' by the dream killers among us; or have dreams eroded by the harsh demands of their environment, situation, and their ongoing involvements.

Surprisingly, the answers we get in life are directly linked to the questions we ask! Ask the right questions and get different, more creative, more fulfilling answers. Often we accept the 'obvious answers' and settle for 'seconds' when we could continue to ask for more and in turn receive even more than we'd ever dreamed possible.

This chapter leads you through a few questions used personally in a search to see my dreams expanded and grounded. This is the place to let your creative visualization skills run amok. Use soft background music to set the atmosphere for your mind to soar, to explore the possibilities these questions may spark. Keep a piece of paper close at hand to capture 'your' insights.

This is a place where you need to be honest, without judgment; a place to let your imagination loose and explore the possibilities. Later we will cover how to integrate this area into your present day reality; to begin seeing your dreams take form as you build solid **Foundations for Success** under them.

Relax! Let your mind flow and wrap your imagination around your 'future'!

What if:

1. I were really in charge of my life, I'd: _____
2. I could do anything, without fear of failure, I'd: _____
3. I had enough money to ensure my basic living needs for a year, I'd: _____
4. I discovered I had the talent or could learn the skills I need to:__, I'd: ___
5. Something I've always wanted to do is: _____

6. IF I could do anything, without limitations, I'd: _____
7. IF spoke as if (I thought) what was saying was important, I'd say: _____
8. I've always wanted to visit: _____
9. I've always wanted to learn to: _____
10. I would like to leave a legacy of: _____
11. IF I could give my family anything, it would be: _____
12. IF I took full responsibilities for my choices, I'd: _____
13. IF I took full responsibility for my actions, I'd: _____
14. IF I were more accepting of: _____, I'd: _____
15. IF I took full responsibilities for my choice of companions, I'd: _____
16. IF I could have any career, without limitations: _____
17. IF I had a dedicated support team to assist me, I'd: _____
18. IF God cared and was willing to help me, I'd: _____
19. My greatest life goal is: _____
20. IF I could accomplish JUST ONE thing before I die, I'd: _____

By now your mind should be whirling with endless possibilities. To explore those possibilities will require a choice of investing time and effort into 'doing your homework'.

To research and refine your dreams using these questions to unlock your creative power; to begin to dream again and to act on those dreams will take courage and commitment. It is so worth it!

Use the **Idea Worksheet** on page 55 to help you focus each dream/goal, explore each idea, and tackle each problem. Use it to help break each down into its component parts and to change them into a realistic goal with specific objectives. It has been designed to facilitate this process and to help you focus and succeed in building your dream; to see your ideas become a reality.

Leaders, Managers, Owners

We'd suggest this book might be a great reference and creative discussion guide for you and your team. Work through it and discuss where it is relevant in your specific needs and culture. Working to create an innovative culture will pay dividends for years to come. We have '*Why Didn't I THINK of That?*' available as a lesser investment E-pub (Kindle) version as well. Why not get each team member their own copy of the print or E-pub version. If you'd like to make a print bulk order, please contact me and we'll work something out, just for you. Email: **bob@ideaman.net www.SuccessPublications.ca**

Unlock Your Creative Potential

"Ideas are the beginning point of all fortunes." Napoleon Hill

Unlocking your 'Creative' potential challenges you to draw from the same 'untapped' creative well that allows you to dream, dare, and declare to the world, *"I DO and will make a difference!"*

We will attempt to 'kick-start' your creativity and challenge your mindsets; to look at what you do, who you are, from a fresh perspective. This 'learning guide' is created to give you some solid ideas to build on in pursuit of that creative and innovative quest.

To truly expand and **Unlock Your 'Creativity' Potential,** explore these ideas:

Learn to tap into your **Creative S.O.U.L.: S**eeker of wisdom; **O**penness to people and ideas; **U**nlimited energy; and a high **L**evel of risk and adventure.

Learn and apply the *creative process* to your situation:
- Preparation
- Incubation
- Illumination
- Implementation or action on your creative thoughts.

Believe in your creative abilities. *Belief precedes creation!*

Don't be afraid to ask 'stupid' questions. There aren't any!

Challenge your assumptions and existing mindsets.

Give your ideas breathing space to germinate and grow.

Read outside your normal zone to expand your mind. *(Try some of my books)*

Mastermind: with a creative, collaborative circle of friends and fellow creative idea seekers.

Travel and be open to explore and expand by truly seeing new ideas.

Learn to explore the World Wide Web. Visit us at: **www.ideaman.net**

Make a conscientious effort to capture, record, and save your ideas. Then Act!

See your **Ideas At Work!** by using the four critical building blocks: Planning, Passion, Persistence, and of course, the Patience to see it through!

Remember to have fun! We learn best in times of enjoyment.

Use 'Thunder-thinking' (brain storming) to get outside your box.

Create a special place or environment that sparks your creativity.

Share and expect synchronicity with the world.

Encourage idea volume generation with all your connections.

Some quick thoughts that might help you crank up the volume and burst your locked in *'I'm not creative'* bubble. I'm confident you'll finish this 6th edition of *'Why Didn't I THINK of That?'* with specific ideas to act on!

As Jacob Bronowski wrote, *"The world can only be grasped by action, not by contemplation...The hand is the cutting edge of the mind."*

Brain Boosters: Give your mind a workout with one of these!

Research and common sense tells us that regular flexing of your creative capacity will make it easier for you to be creative on demand. I've included some brain boosters throughout this book. Enjoy their stimulation!

List as many antonyms (*opposite meaning*) for the word 'narrow'. Eg. Wide.

Close your eyes and write on a piece of paper. Write for a few minutes. Try to do it without consciously thinking about what you are writing. Then open your eyes and 'read' what you have written.

While you are driving to work or home today notice how many people are wearing hats. Count them.

Assume you are a new parent. You must name your child after vegetables. What names would you choose for a boy and for a girl?

"Creativity can solve almost any problem. The creative act, the defeat of habit by originality, overcomes everything."

George Lois

A Creativity Break for Your Team

Finding a way to move your team 'away' from their established routines can work wonders in helping them to unleash their creativity and to enhance and restore their 'on the job' energy.

Routine is the nemesis of creativity! Routine wears down the creative juices over time; slowly killing energy and drive.

Injecting more fun into your day to day operations might be just the tonic to rejuvenate your staff's creativity and on-the-job focus. Innovative companies have taken the lead in this area.

I recall hearing a story about Hewlett-Packard which well illustrates this premise. One morning many members of a Hewlett-Packard team came into work to discover **'subpoenas'** at their desks. They had been summoned to do **'jury duty'** instead of their normal routine. Hewlett-Packard executives planned a **full two-day 'trial'** to involving them (a cross section of their employee base) in deciding the fate of its new business plan.

Employees were divided into three specific teams:

- One team argued against the plan, playing the role of prosecutors
- One team acted as defense attorneys, being its champions
- The third group was sworn in as the jury

After each side had presented its case and argued the merits of their position, the jury rendered its verdict. All of the employees involved in this unique event returned to their 'normal' jobs, energized and excited about the company's new direction. They became its cheerleaders and champions.

What kind of event can you plan to 'jolt' your employees, colleagues, and team members out of their routine? Perhaps we can help you create one? Call us at 1-780-736-0009!

Does this example give you some ideas that might work in your case? If you come up with a creative idea that works, I'd love to hear about it.

"Others have seen what is and asked why. I have seen what could be and asked why not?" **Pablo Picasso**

Creative Freedom

Question everything? Does what you're doing...

+ **Provide enhanced 'value' to the product or customer?**
+ **Improve 'quality'?**
+ **Improve 'productivity' or directly reduce costs?**
+ **Improve 'two-way communication'?**
+ **Improve 'service'**
+ **Add to employee satisfaction, 'motivation' or morale?**
+ **'Empower' your employees to act?**
+ **Encourage 'innovation'?**
+ **Speed up the 'decision-making' process?**
+ **Give customers more 'reasons' to deal with you?**
+ **'Free up time' to more productively sell or service?**

What if it didn't exist?

Is it already being done by someone else?

Is it a 'valid' tradition? Why?

Can another person, department, or company do it better, faster, less expensively, or more easily?

Principles made personal yield powerful results - Ideas At Work!

Creating the freedom you seek challenges you to look at where and what you are currently doing. These questions apply primarily to your career or business role, but many of them can be applied to your life. Answer wisely!

Guess what?

There are people outside of North America... and they are checking out you and your organization!

With the rapid expansion of global internet use, more companies are entering a new arena in marketing and customer service. Is there a fortune to be made for your company? Or is it a black hole to pour money into and hope someone out there is reading it? Worse yet, how are people who live in non-English speaking areas able to take advantage of your services?

Experts predicted Western European Internet users would match or surpass those in North America by the early part of this new century. With 50% of all Internet users estimated to live outside North America, it would make sense to think seriously about how you serve such a diverse mixture of customers. Gee, 24 hour orders and on-line hits seven days a week. Sounds like a dream or nightmare if you're not ready – doesn't it? Can they 'find' you when they are looking for help – either locally or from around the globe?

"Identifying a foreign market is only the first step," say experts. *"Actually tapping into it is a far trickier matter."* Looking at this emerging market from a North American viewpoint won't work to exploit this opportunity. Depending on your company, you may need to set up and implement delivery and warehousing infrastructures with access and understanding of foreign currencies, laws, and business norms. You would need to translate and maintain content that presents or captures the various nuances, subtleties, and tastes of another culture, not your own.

This means getting to understand how the various nationalities you intend marketing to think and shop. Customer service just entered a challenging new era. One way would be to partner with local firms and strategic alliances in the major areas in which you feel you might draw new customers. **What if you want them to visit you here in_____?** Then what?

"European companies, in particular, have an advantage over US companies because they're used to dealing with different cultures and doing business multiple languages," according to **Forrester Research** director John C. McCarthy. *"We (North America) are used to living in a monolithic English cocoon."* The net may cross borders with ease, but capturing different cultures is more than just giving them 'access' to an English speaking site. Expanding your company's presence on-line will be a challenge, but the effort may be worth it. Remember new customers require a new level in customer engagement and that is where your creativity kicks into gear.

A creative approach to writing
using a cartoonist's concept

If you have any amount of writing (business or other) to do as a part of your leadership role or in your organizational process, taking a leaf from the skills or processes used by cartoonists to create their illustrations might be helpful in your creative process.

As a very young boy, we lived in southern California not too far from Disneyland. I remember buying one of those **'learn how to draw books'** *which covered cartooning. They took us through the basics of creating cartoon characters. For example a dog: roughing out an oval for the head and another larger one for the body and then adding more details until the basic drawing started taking shape. I had dreams of working at Disney one day.*

As the cartoon progressed, these initial outlines might be blended with new lines or eliminated altogether. What was important was that those quick broad pencil strokes or lines became the foundation for what would, hopefully, become a colourful, detailed illustration.

Although I did not follow through with the idea of being a cartoonist, I do reflect on the skills learned, as they applied to creativity in my writing. I used these skills 'a lot' when I was designing kitchens. They also provide a creative approach to profitably doing business.

"Bob eating dessert first!"

Whether the writing being done is a simple memo, a white paper or report, a business plan, a mini-book or a full-fledged workbook, or even a hardcover coffee table book; the faded lessons from the creative pages of my *'Learn to Draw Cartoons'* can be invaluable.

These ideas can help you craft your thoughts in creating presentations too! A good writer soon learns that ideas captured or recorded as text notes, or on a computer are very malleable.

When 'inspiration' strikes and an idea appears, you learn to capture those broad strokes of inspiration, perhaps with a few key words, illustrative phrases, or sentence fragments which will help you recall and flesh out the details later.

The important point here is simply capturing the 'essence of the idea', not correct grammar or spelling. It is like the idea generation part in the brainstorming process where the essence is to create and capture the ideas for evaluation, analysis, and application later.

"Writing is simple: capture the ideas or concepts. Make the connections. The rest is editing!" Bob 'Idea Man' Hooey

Much like my amateur attempts at creating shapes as a cartoonist, these initial thoughts or ideas may not survive the finished piece or they may be blended with other ideas, thoughts, and paragraphs as the writing progresses. They do, however, serve a broader purpose, similar to the pencil lines, as they create a starting or launching point or foundation for your written communication. They can provide valuable guides as you move ahead in business, too.

Perhaps you might have to deal with 'writer's block' or uncertainty as to what to put to paper from time to time. Approach your writing project from the cartoonist's view and start with broad, rough stokes of ideas, thoughts, and fragments of thoughts.

Realize you can blend and shape them with an incredible degree of creativity on the canvas of your computer's word processor. Then you can share these thoughts with those you work with, want to inspire, call to action, or simply keep informed. In business, and more so in the role of a business leader, being able to capture and communicate your ideas and thoughts is a success skill that can provide that competitive edge you or your organization needs to win!

"Change comes with such rapidity that businesses must anticipate tomorrow's needs today, because the distinction between today and tomorrow is increasingly blurred. Innovation is the way of life, central to how an organization conducts itself, becomes fundamental to corporate survival."
Nicholas Imparato and Oren Harrari, from *'Jumping the Curve'*

Procter & Gamble adopted UC Berkeley professor **Henry Chesbrough's** *'Open Innovation'* methods in pioneering their Connect and Develop program, where 50% of new product ideas now come from outside the company.

Creativity is 99% perspiration and 1% inspiration
"Whoever said it was going to be easy?"

Bryan Mattimore's excellent creativity book, **'99% Perspiration'** should be in your organization's library. Actually, it should be signed out and being 'worn out' by both you and your team. This kind of instructive reading would be time well spent preparing and priming your creativity pump. This is where the 'creative' and 'profitable' ideas come from in better serving your clients and expanding your career or business. This is where you create ideas to profitably enhance your productivity.

I've adapted this chapter from our *'Create the Future! - Vision and Innovation'* manual as a sampler and perhaps a 'seed' for your success in finding time to more productively grow your own leadership, team, and organization.

Our ongoing success and survival in business is directly dependent on our 'creative ability' to profitably solve the problems in our client's lives and operations. We use our innovative solutions to help make their lives and businesses better. Accessing or tapping into your creativity will be hard work, unless you systemize your approach.

We hear stories of the 'ah-ha' moments in history, business, and science. In reality these 'lightning bolt' or 'light bulb' occurrences nominally come about after many hours of research and applied study into a particular topic.

I know that is how it usually works in my writing and program creation activities. I research, read my brains out, and take copious notes, long before I ever start writing. Then I edit, have other people read and edit, and rewrite. Then I publish and take a breather.

Innovative ideas are sometimes 'mined' from lessons drawn from past failures. Consider **Thomas Edison** and the thousands of attempts to find a sustainable material for the filament for a light bulb.

Take the time to conduct systematic and well-rounded research, coupled with 'mining' the lessons learned from your errors and mistakes. This will help fill your mind with the raw materials necessary for creative process development.

This is, as you guessed, the 'perspiration' part of the creative process and it takes an active investment on your part.

During the 'incubation' period, let your subconscious mind chew on all this material. Let it forge new and varied connections with the seemingly unrelated bits of information. Your subconscious will then send these vague feelings or intuitions to the surface or conscious mind. The creative leader knows to capture these random thoughts, however vague, impractical, or wild for later evaluation and analysis.

Be open and accessible to all ideas – regardless of size

I've seen many people fall into the trap of waiting for the 'big idea' – a completely novel idea for a product, project, or service. They sit and wait for sudden inspiration or brilliant flashes of insight. Many are still waiting. Focusing on big ideas, we can easily become blinded from seeing smaller, otherwise 'good' and 'valuable' solutions.

Like the story I heard of an employee in the **GAP** *mailroom who noticed several packages being couriered to the same address. He checked into it, compiled them into one package with instructions on distribution at the receiving end. His 'small' change in process saved his company tens of thousands of dollars each year.*

While not as flashy or showy, these smaller insights and innovative ideas often represent very workable and profitable options. Some can even lay the foundation for other great ideas or new products and services.

Encourage your team to capture or share their ideas with you and investigate all of the options contained. Consider that the 'original' idea for the $1 billion dollar a year, **Levi Strauss** Dockers line came from one of their employees in Argentina (who worked on the docks).

Time to sweat – perspiration activities

What can you do to fertilize your mind for enhanced brainstorming, or thunder thinking, as I like to call it? *(Thunder thinking™ – when lightning strikes!)*

What kind of research or mental preparation or 'perspiration' activities will help you and your fellow leaders and professionals?

Ideas applied successfully by creative thinkers

- Visit authoritative web sites and learn how to use search engines to conduct in-depth on-line research
- Challenge your existing assumptions and mindsets. No sacred cows!
- Remember to have fun! We learn best during times of enjoyment.
- Use Google's news alert program to keep you informed on selected areas (other search engines and web based programs will provide this type of material, often on a daily basis.) I have several news topics on leadership, creativity, and innovation and get emails with links to those stories on a daily basis. Primes my pump!
- Read books and magazine articles on the topic you are studying.
- Map out the information you need and potential sources where you might find it. Then go looking!
- Ask carefully crafted open-ended questions to draw out or elicit the most usable and rich information of experts in the area of your study. They will often be able to 'kick start' your creativity, give you a heads up, and advance your process to the next level.
- Don't be afraid to ask seemingly stupid questions – there aren't any!
- Learn to apply the four step creative process to fully explore your ideas: preparation, incubation, illumination, and, of course, implementation or taking action on the idea.

Kraft Dinner – now you're cooking!

The story behind this decade-by-decade best-seller, as I learned it, happened following the war when Kraft Foods had pallets of their powered cheese packages (used by servicemen during the war) sitting 'unsold' in warehouses across the country. One particular east-coast manager was 'actually' selling out and headquarters sent someone to find out his secret.

As I heard the story, he creatively took the powered cheese packages, bundled each with a package of pasta and called it **Kraft Dinner**. Love the story and the creativity behind it. What do you have and what can you combine with it to make it more attractive or appetising to your clients?

Another creative example: **Lego Toys** *(Denmark) taps into crowd-sourcing to inspire ideas from customers to help their 180 designers. Submissions that receive 10,000 plus votes from Lego site visitors are reviewed by Lego designers. If your model is chosen for production you will receive 1% of your toy's revenue. How cool is that!* **Can you see how to tap into your client's mind to improve your business?**

Growing profitably to the next level (using innovation)

Is your organization stagnating? Are you finding it a challenge just to keep up with the regular demands made on your team? How do you keep growing? **Growing your people will result in growing your organization.** Making innovation an integral embedded process may just be the answer. After all, you have a process for almost everything else don't you? *'Prepare Yourself to WIN!'* by investing time and resources in equipping your team to profitably grow.

A book by **Robert B. Tucker** shed some light and offered us solid advice on how to do this. In *'Driving Growth Through Innovation'*, Robert outlined a synthesis of options based on what leading companies like Proctor & Gamble, Colgate-Palmolive, Shell, and Citigroup do to encourage growth and earning rates through applied innovation. He described how they have been able to bring new ideas to life for *'greater speed, payback, and more consistent momentum'*. What sets these corporate role models apart is their ability to include everyone throughout the organization in the innovation process. They are able to uncover 'unmet' client needs or desires, create and produce prototype ideas in a short time frame, and assess feasibility quickly. We'll talk more about that later. *My thoughts on his innovative ideas below.*

Organic or inward 'growth' will become more critical in the years to come. It will come from applied innovation, not cost cutting bottom line oriented activities. These are always important, but they don't drive top line growth or sustain profitability. They will be counter-productive, if not handled correctly. Investing in innovation and teaching everyone on your team these principles of applied innovation, as shared by **Robert B. Tucker**, will bring you the desired ROI you seek and perhaps the 'real' top-line growth as well.

Tucker's 5 Principles of Applied Innovation

Approach innovation as a discipline. Teach your team to think *'through'* their ideas and how to understand which ones are in alignment with your organization's visions, goals, mission statements, or principles. Remember, you get better at something with guided practice, so encouragement works, even if the initial ideas need work. Show your team how to champion and sell their ideas and where they can go (*hopefully to you*) for coaching and encouragement, as well as how to build creative coalitions of support.

Approach innovation comprehensively. If you want innovation to become an ingrained mindset in your organization, don't let it be confined to one department or an 'elite' group of high performers.

Innovation performance needs to be a part of every job description, and every manager or supervisor's evaluation. **Recruit for this skill** - beef up your innovation muscles with creative team members.

Promote from this perspective to send a consistent and positive message. Innovation must encompass new product development, services, training and development, processes, customer service, strategies, finance and business models, markets, and distribution channels. Each is important to succeed.

Innovation must incorporate a systematic, organized, and continued search for new opportunities and venues to explore. Promote a deeper understanding of social, demographic, and technological changes in your search for the possibilities in your future. Why not challenge your team to become 'trend spotters' who search for disruptive technologies, new innovations and inventions; and perhaps even wacky ideas that might contain the seeds of innovation you need? Mining the future from the minds of today!

Everyone in the organization must be involved in innovation. Ensure your team builds an 'idea management' system to capture ideas from the rank and file, not just your management personnel. Good innovative ideas often come from the fringe of your team, the ones you normally wouldn't ask, who see areas of improvement or new services but may be too shy to share. Make it a point to draw out their input, insight, and experience. They may have encountered something with a client that could provide the innovative genesis of a new line or profitable service addition.

Innovation must be customer centered to be profitable. You can't always depend on the insights provided from your clients. Sometimes they don't know or recognize what they need or want until you show it to them. **A focus of innovation** to make their lives better, in service, in selection, in making it easier for them to do business with you, and in how you handle their concerns, problems, and complaints will do wonders. Creating *visible* value for the client is the only sure route to continued success.

Client focused innovation is more profitable as it deals with the 'top-line' of your business. Innovation to shore up your bottom line also enables you to grow and put those 'liberated' resources into growth, promotion, and performance enhancement. **Listen to your clients**, you might learn something that could provide a new or unconventional way of doing business and continue to earn theirs. Taking time to understand these five principles of applied innovation will help your team develop a strategy for innovation to guide your organization through good and bad times.

From 'KAI-ZEN' to 'I CAN!'
Improvement = Consistent commitment to good change

Kai = *change*   Zen = *good*
When they are used together = *improvement*

Kai-zen came to popularity in North America during the mid-1980's, after becoming an integral part of the Japanese management theory. Western management consultants used it to embrace a wide range of management practices, which were regarded as primarily Japanese. These practices were thought to be the secrets of the strength of Japanese companies in the areas of continual improvement rather than innovation.

According to this theory, the strength of Japanese organizations lay in their attention to process rather than results. They also concentrated the team efforts to continually improve imperfections at each stage of the process. According to them, over the long-term, the final result was more reliable, of better quality, more advanced and attractive to clients, and less expensive than Western Management practices.

Its roots however are from an American influence following the 2nd World War. **General Douglas MacArthur** approached several leading US experts to visit Japan to advise them on how to proceed with rebuilding their country and their economy. One such expert was **Dr. Edwards Deming (1900-1993).**

He initially came to Japan to conduct a census, but noticed the newly emerging industries were having difficulty. He had been involved in reducing waste in US War manufacturing and drew on that experience to offer his advice. By the 1950's, he was a regular visitor, offering advice to Japanese manufacturers that were having challenges in terms of raw materials, components, and investment; additionally suffering from low morale in the nation and workforce. By the 1970's, many of Japan's leading organizations had embraced Dr. Deming's key points for management. Most are as valid today as they were a half-century ago.

Key points that relate specifically to the concept called Kai-zen

- An improved philosophy to effectively deal with change and client needs.
- Constant pursuit of purpose required for improvement of products and services.
- Improving every process for planning, production, and service.

- Instituting or embedding on-going, on the job training for all staff using a variety of methods and ideas.
- Instituting and supporting leadership that is aimed and focused on helping people do a better job. *(Isn't that the true purpose of 21ˢᵗ Century leadership and management?)*
- Breaking down the barriers and boundaries that exist within departments and people. *(GE's CEO, Jack Welsh took this one on personally in his style of management.)*
- Encouraging education for the self-improvement of every member of the organization.
- Top management is committed to improve '*all*' these points, specifically quality and leadership.

Adapting the Kai-zen attitude to our western way of doing business requires a 'major change in corporate culture' – **creating a corporate culture that**:

- Admits openly and honestly there are problems and challenges.
- Encourages a positive, collaborative, consultative attitude to solving or overcoming them.
- Actively 'devolves' responsibility to the most appropriate or effective level. The person who is in the best position to deal with the challenge or problem needs to have the time, the tools, and the authority to do so.
- Promotes continuous skills-based training and development of attitudes.

The Japanese approach has embedded Kai-zen in its hierarchical structural, although it gives substantially more responsibilities within certain fixed boundaries.

Key features of this management approach and focus are:

- Attention to process, rather than results: Analyze every part of the process down to the smallest detail, with a view to improving them. Looks at how employee's actions, equipment, and materials can be improved.
- Cross-functional management: Management team has an expanded focus to help improve the process and the skills of the people outside the typical western turf wars.
- Use of quality circles: and other tools to support their commitment to continuous improvement.

A range of tools have been developed, along the KAI-ZEN concept, to assist companies to make tangible improvements:

- **Quality Control Circles**: groups of people whose primary focus and purpose is to continually improve quality.
- **Process-oriented management**: more attention focused on the 'how' (the process) rather than the 'what' (the task).
- **Visible management**: top executives are being seen, 'walking the job' (management by walking around) and being available to 'see' and consult on each stage of the process.
- **Cross-functional management**: working across functional divides and typical barriers or boundaries to provide more unity, sense of team, and a wider vision that engages and involves everyone.
- **Just-in-time management**: control of stock and other materials and components to avoid unnecessary expenditures.
- **PDCA**: a process of **P**lan, **D**o, **C**heck, **A**ct to assist in solving challenges.
- **Statistical process control**: enable each machine operator or member of a team to control and measure quality at each stage of the process.

In the Japanese approach to Kai-zen, all of these tools are used in a 'holistic' manner. Contrast this to the current western approach where some of these tools are individually introduced as the 'answer' to every problem or challenge; without consideration of the context within which they were designed to work effectively.

Perceived benefits of this Kai-zen type of approach:

- Can lead to a reduction of 'wasted' time and resources.
- Can increase productivity.
- Relatively easy to introduce – requires no major capital investment.
- Can lower the break-even point.
- Enables organizations to react quickly to market changes.
- Appropriate for fast and slow economies as well as growing or mature markets.

However, we face **challenges when introducing Kai-zen** into the western management mind-set.

It can be difficult to achieve Kai-zen in practice, as it requires a complete or major change in attitude and culture. It needs the energy and commitment of all employees. It also requires a substantive investment of time by leaders and their respective teams. Leaders need to 'slow down' and invest their energy to make this mindset work.

It can be difficult to maintain enthusiasm for several reasons. Some see Kai-zen as a threat to their jobs; poor ideas tend to be put forward along with good ideas, which can at times be de-motivating; by implication, there is never complete satisfaction.

Continuous improvement is not sufficient or a stand-alone approach in itself. Major innovation is still needed. There is a danger of becoming 'evolutionary' in focus to the exclusion of being 'revolutionary' or innovation sensitive. Both concepts are important to growth and sustainability.

In this turbulent, global economy, organizations need to look seriously at any and all methods, tools, techniques, and training processes that might help in this quest for growth. Kai-zen's step-by-step approach is in direct contrast to the great leaps forward many organizations experience via the innovation avenue.

It is almost as though we need to develop a 'bi-focal' approach and viewpoint, which is one that encompasses steady, continuous improvement of current processes, products, and services; while looking for and encouraging creativity and innovation in moving the organization to the next level. *I do this in the development of my various training programs and publications.*

Kai-zen should free up time for senior managers to think about the long-term future of the organization, look for new opportunities, and move to a concentration on 'strategic' issues. Kai-zen can support improvement of 'existing' activities; but it will not provide the impetus for the innovation process, which often provides our great leaps forward. Again, a balanced approach is called for here.

- It is the role of 'strategic' leadership to take responsibility for the implementation of an effective corporate mission (purpose or soul), reward, and the organizational structure.
- It is the responsibility of 'tactical and strategic' managers to model and practice sound leadership, to promote good teamwork, and to work to ensure everyone understands their roles and the process itself.
- It is the responsibility of 'everyone' in the organization (from front-line to senior management), to measure themselves and their teams; to identify in quantifiable, measurable terms, areas for improvement; and to generate ideas to change practice and procedures. Then, continue measurement to ensure this improvement has been achieved, recorded, and celebrated.
- Each time it is measured, it can be analyzed and a new standard achieved or set and measured. This is the cycle of continual improvement. (I CAN!)

A typical or **suggested 'cycle' or process**:

Generate ideas
Evaluate ideas
Decide on action
Plan implementation
Design measurement system
Take action (key)
Set new standard
Measure
Analyze
Define problem/desired state
Identify areas for improvement
Generate ideas

Everyone on your team needs to be 'totally' committed to this cycle of continuous improvement. Each team member must be given the knowledge, skills, and tools to be able to participate fully and enthusiastically. They need to participate, not only within their own respective teams; but also across the organization as a whole and as a part of a cross-functional team.

For this to become a reality, work must be undertaken to reinforce, encourage, or build the confidence within your staff to take on greater responsibility and make decisions for themselves.

This was the underlying foundation to the work we did in writing and creating *'The Brick Way – It's about ALL of us'* for a major Canadian Retailer. We wanted to send and support the message of each member of their 6000 plus member team taking additional responsibilities and personal leadership over their respective roles. We wanted to instill a new culture and work to create a *'Company of Leaders'*.

This reinforcement is crucial to Kai-Zen's success. In addition to specific skills training and use of tools and knowledge, it is important for us to work on the 'climate for change'; to ensure it is embedded in our corporate culture.

The core values within a Kai-zen based approach to which each of us can aspire are:

44

Trust and respect for every member of the team across the organization, not just his or her own team. (Not just their department, their own specialization, expertise, or level.) Each individual on a team should be able to openly admit any mistakes or failings they've made or exist in their role, and work on doing a better job the next time. Responsibility is an individual commitment. Progress is impossible without the ability to admit, learn from, and move forward from mistakes.

A few years back, I listened to '*A Power Talk*' CD from **Tony Robbins**, in which he shared his concept of 'CANI' (Constant and Never Ending Improvement) for use in our day-to-day lives and roles as leaders. He was quite passionate about his commitment to this concept and for its implementation in our daily lives. He advocated a commitment to constant and never ending improvement.

I'd like to take a 'robbins-esque' approach and challenge each of you to take a moment to digest what we've discussed about this transplanted US – filtered through Japan approach to management, as a part of your leadership role. I reworded it to a more positive focused **'I CAN'** acronym. **Improvement is continual and never ending.**

If you and your team are going to be successful in taking your organization to the next level of growth, each of you will need to get a firm foundation and focus on the process of Kai-zen style continual improvement. This is in addition to your personal leadership in applied innovation or **Ideas At Work!** - as they apply to your changing roles and the teams you seek to lead.

My challenge for each of you: **Develop an 'I CAN!' approach** and attitude to your leadership and team management and to equip and inspire those you would seek to lead. 'Improvement is continual and never ending' and it starts with me!'

You can use this **'I CAN' Kai-Zen based focus** in your quest to free up time that you choose to reinvest in the lives and skills of those you lead. Enjoy the journey! In the 'Kai-zen' or 'I CAN!' world, the journey is the goal and provides the sense of achievement and satisfaction. It really works for top performing leaders and their teams as they remain committed to continual improvement in how they leverage their time and enhance their productivity.

Check out www.mindsnacks.com for some amazing apps you can download. You can learn a language and educational tips in your free time. Creative use of your phone to learn.

The 21ˢᵗ Century version of the 3 R's

When my mom went to school, the **3 R's used to be: Reading, writing and 'rithmetic.** We need to redefine them to deal with the complex challenges we face today. Many innovations are not 'entirely' new; in fact, many represent new combinations, applications, or modifications of current, existing services, products, technologies, or materials.

I've done this with my writing and programs by drawing from previous programs or writing (articles, books) in the creation of something more adaptive or relevant to my audiences. In fact, we drew from some of our other publications, class notes, surveys, and resources for this revamped 6ᵗʰ edition of *'Why Didn't I THINK of That?'*

Not re-inventing the wheel each time, but taking it a step up or further in the development of its use and scope is a good way to 'leverage your time' and expertise. Fortunately, computers, word processing, visual outlining, or diagramming programs make it easier to gather, analyze, and manipulate information fragments into new combinations or versions for use.

This allows you to apply **these 21ˢᵗ Century 3 R's in your creative process**.

- **Research**, retrieve, and record information.
- **Review** and revise the information you gather.
- **Recombine** or re-use ideas – make new associations between the idea fragments of information you've gathered.

Tips to help facilitate your creative process

With the proper preparation, any one of your team members can experience an 'ah-ha' moment. Properly applied, each team member can accomplish it. It takes training, but it is not something only an Einstein would be able to do.

Know where to look for information. Love learning – become a sponge for information on your topic or field of study. Develop the skill of asking incisive, well thought-out, open-ended questions that draw out the information, the insights, and the wisdom of those you approach.

Experiment with mind mapping or other right brain stimulation tools to map out your assumptions, questions, insights, concerns, and needs for more information.

During the interim (time delay or pause) between your 'Thunder-thinking'™ and specific brainstorming sessions, remain open for additional insights. Be a mental sponge starting with your industry or profession and flowing outward, upward, into cross-functional disciplines, business, social, or other areas. The insight you seek may not be found in the place you live or work, but it is out there.

Cultivate an 'insight-outlook'. Be open to consider information, insights, trends, and other data mined from multiple perspectives and personal experience. Work to identify and understand the inferences, underlying trends or connections they may contain and how they might pertain or impact what you are working on in your study.

Secret Selling Tips... Creativity can be a service focus

A number of years ago, I had lunch with the CEO of a large Canadian retail firm. I had worked with them for a number of years; training their VPs, helping create a book to reinforce their culture, as well as writing for their internal magazine. I had also coached and worked with their founder, **Bill Comrie**, helping him craft numerous presentations he needed to make as he garnered award after award including an honorary doctorate.

As we came to the finish of our lunch, **Kim Yost** mentioned he needed to find a way to help his 1500 sales people across Canada become more productive, focused, and profitable. We brainstormed ideas and in less than 15 minutes had outlined the basic idea for what would soon become our online sales coaching and training **www.SecretSellingTips.com**. We launched the English version a month later and the French version shortly after that.

I approached this challenge as a way to better serve this particular leader, who had become a good friend and mentor. What I didn't see, at that moment, was this customer service focus would lead to a completely new, profitable, on-line business adventure for us. A few months after the launch, he invited me to share what we'd done with nine of his counterparts south of the border. They met in Chicago three times a year to share 'best ideas' and I was to be his best idea that year. We presented what we were doing and four companies immediately signed up their entire sales teams too. Wow! This simple creative service-based idea started generating $30-50K a year.

What can you do to better serve your clients? Where can you tap into your creative genius to make their lives and businesses better?

The importance of a professional strategic development plan

Whether you are in business for yourself or work for a living, having a strategic plan covering your professional or business development is essential to your long term success or employability. Failure to plan is truly as we've heard, planning to fail! **This is particularly important if you want to create innovative ways to attract and retain clients and customers.**

A good plan incorporates several basic components: (see page 55)

- A clear definition of the ultimate objective in mind. **Conceive it complete!**
- A good solid foundation built on understanding what is required to make it happen by **doing your homework.**
- An **ACTION** plan with specific goals and objectives tied to specific timelines and checkpoints to make revisions along the way.

How do you define your idea or 'ultimate' objective as it relates to your value-added business or career? A little free flow idea generation or creative, blue sky 'dreaming' works. Ask yourself - some **'What if?'** questions to unlock your creativity and help **unlock your full service potential.**

- What if I could do anything without fear of failure? I'd _____
- If I had enough money to ensure my basic living for a year I'd _____
- If I discovered I had the talent, or could learn the skills I need to: _____
  I'd _____

The answers to these types of questions will give you a glimpse into what you'd really like to do with your life and what may need to change or adapt to get there. After you've defined your ultimate desire, then what? Well, now it's time to start doing your homework and find out exactly what is needed to make it happen or prepare you to act.

Then comes the fun part - setting **specific action plans** in place to accomplish goals and objectives that will lead you to your ultimate desire - a whole bunch of happy satisfied customers who love you and tell the world about you! The key is to ensure that your goals are clear and specific and can be broken down into even more specific objectives.

Any action plan is only as good as its implementation and accountability. This means setting specific time lines for starting and completion of each step. It also means having numerous built-in checkpoints to allow you to monitor your progress and make any fine tuning adjustments or course corrections to the plan as you move into its implementation.

Are you are serious about bringing a creative approach to your career, team, or organization? INVESTING the necessary time to do some serious thinking about what you want to accomplish, when, and why is essential. Success doesn't come by accident - it requires strategic planning followed by implementation on your ACTION plan.

Studies have shown that visual disorder can make you more creative.

I thought I was just 'messy' when working on a creative project or writing. Hmm.

According to an Inc. magazine article, this is demonstrable in structured experiments.

Kathleen Voss, a marketing professor for the University of Minnesota (with an extensive psychology background) recently told a Yale School of Management audience about repeated experiments that have demonstrated you can actually get a creative boost when you work in a 'messy' space. Her research was individual vs. team based. She stated that 'messy' and 'tidy' each have their place in business settings. For example, visual disorder might facilitate brainstorming while a quick meeting where an immediate decision is required might work better in a neater setting.

In one experiment (later verified by Northwestern University) teams in 'messy' rooms were on average rated 28% more creative than their counterparts in tidy rooms. All ideas were rated by independent judges. In addition, when the 'highly creative' ideas were analyzed it was found that the messy room subjects came up with nearly 5 times the number vs. their tidy room counterparts.

PROBLEMS

"Each problem has hidden in it an opportunity so powerful that it literally drawfs the problem. The greatest success stories were created by people who recognized a problem and turned it into an opportunity."
Joseph Sugarman

"When you approach a problem, strip yourself of preconceived opinions and prejudice, assemble and learn the facts of the situation, make the decision which seems to you to be the most honest, and stick to it."
Chester Bowles

"I am grateful for all my problems. After each one was overcome, I became stronger and more able to meet those that were still to come. I grew in all my difficulties."
J.C. Penny

Problems are a part of life and even more so of being in business. Problems may be why you exist. How you view them and deal with them is a pivot point for your long term profitability and even survival. The following pages take you through effectively dealing with these opportunities (problems) in your life.

So you have a problem... that's great!

So you have a problem, that's great! Whoa? Some of you are thinking, *"Are you crazy?"* Actually... NO! Someone once told me that **"I'd get paid or determine my value, by my ability to solve problems"**.

If it was that 'easy', everyone would be doing it, and the competition would be intense. But, as most customers will tell you, most businesses are not in the problem-solving field. Your ability to solve your client's problems will be directly related to the number of sales and continued growth of your firm. The more successfully and **creatively you solve these problems**, the more referrals and fans you'll see. The more productive you are personally in being a solution oriented owner, manager, or employee, the more dramatically it will impact your paycheck and career path.

I've learned a **simple 4-stage process for dealing with problems**. This is an effective way to deal creatively with customer complaints and concerns as well as other areas of your business and life. These ideas also work with creative and strategic planning or in everyday problem solving.

Since many of my clients and audiences have a need to be effective in dealing with their clients or customers, I've written from that perspective.

1. Invest time making sure you **UNDERSTAND** the problem.

2. The key to understanding is to **IDENTIFY** the real cause.

3. Take time to fully explore and **DISCUSS** possible solutions.

4. Take action to **SOLVE** or resolve the problem.

Creative client engagement is a commitment to go through this process with your clients. After the problem has been successfully resolved, **go the extra mile**. By that I mean 'do' something unexpected to assist the client or to show them you appreciate the opportunity to fix the problem and prove your commitment to his well-being. This will help turn an angry or frustrated client into a fan or better yet a champion for you and your business.

Stage One: Understanding the problem. Often a problem is a perception of a difference of what we expected to happen and what actually happened. Here are three action steps to help.

1. Gather **ALL** the facts. Be thorough and investigate. Let the client talk!

2. Listen carefully and don't be defensive. Wait until they've finished talking and ask more questions to draw them out to find out their **REAL** concerns.

3. Rephrase or repeat the problem back to the client to make sure you've heard it correctly and understand what needs to be resolved. Agree at this stage.

It's important at this point to ensure you don't fall into the trap of denying or trying to avoid the problem. Don't blame or attack someone else. Don't demonstrate the same negative emotions in response to a customer's complaint. Just listen and calmly gather the facts!

Stage Two: Identify the Cause of the Problem. You might ask yourself or your client a few questions to find out what may have caused the problem.

1. **What has happened?** Listen and ask questions. Undertake a true assessment of the current situation.

2. **What should have happened?** Ask questions and listen carefully. Was perception a problem?

3. **What went wrong?** This is where you start partnering with the client.

Keep in mind the true cost of an unhappy client. What future purchases could you expect from this client? What future business could this client influence? What does the problem at hand cost to rectify?

Problems generally often fall into 4 major areas:

1. **Mechanics or Function** - product or service failed to work as expected.

2. **Assembly or use** - someone didn't use it correctly or put it together incorrectly.

3. **The People Factor** - we make mistakes in how we do something or how we deal with a client.

4. **Client EGO** - how this PROBLEM makes them look (good or bad) in their eyes and the eyes of their friends and families.

Stage Three: Explore and DISCUSS possible solutions. This is possibly the most critical part in the client satisfaction/problem solving process. Here is where we need to fully focus and objectively look at the challenge we've partnered with the client to solve. Here are three action steps.

1. **Suggest options.** Take time to explore ALL the options that might effectively help solve this problem or at least minimize the impact.

2. **Ask your customer for their ideas.** Very often, they have a solution in mind or have some good input that will help you mutually resolve it to their satisfaction. If they are a partner in the decision, they will help make it work and will be more inclined to be happy with the results. Their satisfaction will result in referrals for you!

3. **Agree on the best solution or course of action.** After you've fully explored the options, make sure you both agree on what you will do and when in order to resolve it. THEN DO IT!

Stage Four: Take ACTION to resolve the problem. This is the completion stage that builds a foundation for a potential long-term relationship with your 'formerly' dissatisfied client. Make this a priority focus for your firm. Once you've agreed on what needs to be done, move heaven and earth to do it and do it better and quicker than you've promised.

Remember, they are watching to make sure you were serious about making them happy. This is your chance to 'prove' your commitment. **Again, three simple action steps.**

1. Physically remove the cause of the problem and/or take steps to retrain if it involves personnel.

2. Take corrective action to substitute, replace, or repair the product or service.

3. Ask the client if they are satisfied with the changes and action you've taken.

Go the extra mile! This is where you cement the relationship by doing something extra, something totally unexpected by the client. Show them you care and are concerned about the inconvenience they've experienced.

Use your complaints as a source of product or service development. Each one is an opportunity for you to learn how to better serve your clients, refine your service, or improve your product in the market place.

This is also an opportunity to expand your business or service by using solutions as stepping stones or business building blocks.

Yesterday's problems are today's new creations and improved products or services. Want to be a creativity leader? Then learn from each lesson your clients give you. This is an opportunity for you to build a strong foundation for success. **Don't miss the lesson. It might be a 'v-e-r-y' valuable one!**

A personal note from Bob

I trust we've been able to share creative approaches to problem solving or strategic planning in this updated *'Why Didn't I THINK of That?'* I appreciate the opportunity to exercise my creativity and learn together with my audiences. Often, the lessons we discuss and the ideas generated help me refine my approach and my program content.

I would challenge you to use these tips and techniques in your day-to-day operations, as well as in your personal life. I trust you'll find them helpful.

Remember there is 'always' a creative solution! Share these ideas with your clients and co-workers, so they can take advantage of ways to make their lives more productive and less stressful. As you continue to read and re-read, focus on the ones that might serve you best as you begin to reframe your approach to problems that inevitably appear in your life and career. I hope you enjoy it.

One of the challenges of speaking within a time frame and having a topic that has so many variables to discuss is covering the most relevant material. That is one of the reasons for developing these books and learning guides to help my audience members following a presentation.

Brain Boosters: (take a minute and play with one or two)

Think of three legal things you could do to get on the evening news.

All college freshmen are required to take an entry level course in creativity. What are the main things taught in this course?

List three questions you would like to ask your boss. Whatever three questions you ask, your boss also gets to ask you.

A new movie is coming out called the 'Enablers'. What is the story line?

Bob's Idea/Problem-solving Worksheet

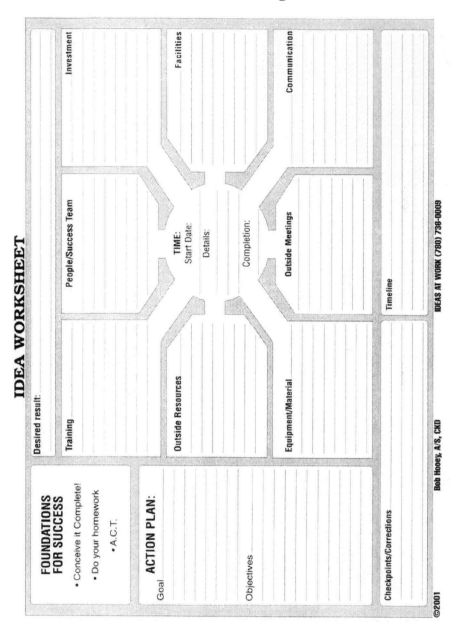

Let's explore how to get the most out of this problem-solving creativity worksheet. It was professionally designed as an easy-use form with built-in questions to assist you in making your goal a reality or in solving your problem.

This worksheet was originally designed to help my consulting clients and myself focus our thoughts and to break down problems; or help us 'Thunder Think' (brainstorm) our way through idea generation to idea application. It is shared as a reference for your continued success. I would encourage you to actively share these principles with your friends, family, co-workers, and clients. The worksheet was designed for your personal use only and is protected by copyright.

Visit **www.SuccessPublications.ca/Think.htm** to download your own personal copy. Feel free to use as many as you need as you tackle challenges.

Foundations for Success are highlighted in the upper left-hand corner to assist your progress. Each part of the worksheet is designed to help you build on these Foundations for Success. Make sure you clearly define 'exactly' what you want to achieve or resolve. This is a critical step in achieving your goal, birthing your idea or dream, or in eventually resolving your problem.

Desired result (what do you want to accomplish?)

CONCEIVE IT COMPLETE

What do I mean by that? Something I've learned from several sources is the importance of good visualization. In order for you to successfully reach your desired result, you must be able to visualize it as though it already exists or is resolved. The more accurately you can *describe it, feel it, touch it, taste it, smell it, or define it*, the better chance you have of seeing it come into being.

Often one or two short sentences will suffice to define it at this point. It will be helpful as you work through the homework section to refer back to your desired result, as you've defined it, when answering the various questions.

You may find it evolving as you work through this process. That's ok! In fact that evolution is part of the process and part of the rationale of working through all of these questions. One of the biggest obstacles to success or idea implementation is an accurate and current goal. Too many have totally missed the mark by being 'off the mark' when they began their journey.

DO YOUR HOMEWORK

Training

What training will you or your co-workers need to reach your desired result?

Will you need to go back to school, take a night course, or get on the job training to gain the knowledge and skills required for successfully reaching your goal? Can you get Internet based training or special training from your professional association?

People/Success Team

What support would you or your co-workers need? Who do you need to recruit to augment the skills you already possess? Do you need partners? Do you need additional employees? Do you need aligned professionals? Do you need tradesman or technical assistance to build a facility or special programming?

Investment

What are you willing to invest in the accomplishment of your desired result? What will it take to make it a reality? Will you need to arrange financing? What type, how much, from whom? How much time will you or your team need to invest in this pursuit? How will you schedule this time? Time and money are both valuable commodities. Invest them wisely!

Facilities

What facilities do you need to achieve or launch this desired result? Do you need an office or extra work space, warehouse, storefront, or a mall location? Can you telecommute from home or a satellite office? Can you co-op space to start and expand as you grow?

One of the growing trends in North America is the independent contractor. With so many people making the move or having their former employers 'encouraging them to make the move', you'll be in good company. Who can you co-op with for the facilities you both need to launch and establish a profitable business?

Communication

What do you need for effective communication tools or skills? Do you need a separate phone line, cell phone, fax line, Internet access, or post office box? Have you learned how to promote your program or desired result by the effective use of personal contact promotion and media management?

Will you need to learn how to present your thoughts and needs accurately and with impact through public speaking?

Do you know where to find a **Toastmasters Club** in your area? Simply log onto: **www.toastmasters.org.** Have you visited them yet? Tell them Bob Hooey, DTM, Accredited Speaker said hello!

Outside meetings/groups

Will you need to conduct meetings with other people? Will you need to join outside community or trade associations to network and promote your desired result? When do they meet? How much will it cost to join? What qualifications do you need to gain membership? What will you gain from this association? Is there a professional association in your field or industry?

One of the best things I've done for my speaking and training career was my decision to join **NSA** and later **CAPS** and get involved with speakers and leaders from around the globe. I have been amazed at how often someone 'more established' has taken the time to share a success secret or some critical information to building a solid foundation for my success. Thanks!

Equipment/ material

What specific equipment or materials do you need to launch or achieve your desired result? Do you need to buy it, borrow it, lease it, or get the use of it after hours from a friend or fellow worker? What do you already have that you can use? Is it suitable for your needs, with the option of expanding or adding to it at a later date?

Outside Resources

What specific resources do you need to reach your desired result? Where can you get them? Do you need people or information resource support? Who and what do you need? What resources do you already have to bring to the table? Can you barter or trade services to get what you need?

Time

When do you plan to start working on your desired result? Give as many details as necessary to assist in setting a realistic time line for tracking later. When do you need to have it completed? How long will it take to complete your homework or research? How long will it take to arrange the financing, assemble the team, find the location, etc?

How long will it need to gain approvals from the appropriate authorities or management? Do you, your team, your suppliers, or strategic alliances have any specific deadlines that affect your decisions or investments?

A.C.T. NOW!

A.C.T. now by setting a realistic **A**ction Plan with built in **C**heckpoints or course corrections and a specific **T**imeline.

Goal

Take your research and transfer your desired results to a **S**pecific, **M**easurable, **A**ction-oriented, **R**ealistic, **T**imely goal. **ACT SMART!** Write down your goal with as much detail and as focused as possible.

Objectives

Focus the power of your goal by setting out specific objectives to make it reality. Again, the more definitive you can make them, the better chance of eventual success.

Checkpoints/corrections

Build in specific checkpoints where you can pause and re-evaluate your progress and make any necessary course corrections needed to successfully reach your goal. This is where you really build your desired result. Be ready to react to and avoid detours, roadblocks, and idea and dream killers. Keep focused on your desired result. Revisit it often to keep in mind why you are going down this road and what awaits you at its completion. Don't be afraid to alter or change direction to reach your ultimate goal and the desired result. Course corrections and changes are a natural part of seeing your desired result come to fruition.

Timeline

Set specific, measurable timelines for your progress and achievement. Break it down into segments *(your homework will be critical at this point)* which can be charted and scheduled. Don't be afraid to change or adapt your timeline to react to specific needs, new developments, or information you may encounter along the way. Your idea worksheet is simply a guideline to assist you - not restrict you - in the development and accomplishments you desire.

Team notes

After you've done your homework and mapped out your journey, give some careful thought to the team who will help you reach your desired result or ultimate goal. We don't do it alone and more often do it more effectively and accurately with the help of other like-minded individuals along the way.

Gathering a group of positive, encouraging people, who themselves are working on a desired result of their own can be extremely helpful. They may be fellow workers, people from different departments, divisions, suppliers, competitors, or clients. The varied strengths and support of such a success team will help keep you focused and on track when you encounter the inevitable tests and trials enroute to reaching your ultimate goal.

See Creating a Mastermind Alliance or Success Team section on page 99 for more information.

Putting it all together. Using this Idea Worksheet will allow you to ask yourself the probing or insightful questions that will allow you to build a solid foundation under your idea or solution to your problem.

A few more thoughts on leveraging technology

SMART Cell phones – can be a productivity tool, **or** a major waste of time depending on how you use them. Using your dead time to return calls or keep in touch with the office, your family, or clients can be a great use of your time. Using it to allow clients to get back to you when you need to hear from them or in cases of crisis is great, too. Use SMART phones to check and answer email while waiting. There are numerous APS available, with more being added daily. Find which ones will creatively add to your productivity or allow you to use your time effectively.

*I quite frequently use mine when sitting in an airport to call back clients and have actually completed deals on the tarmac. It also allows me to move my 'office' to a nearby coffee shop for a change of scenery and pace. My amazing and creative wife, **Irene** has been teaching me to use Google maps to help me find places I need to visit and to plan my driving route. I have even trained my phone to allow me to use voice commands for hands free calling. I have numerous books downloaded so I am never without something to read.*

Creativity Columbo Style

One of the biggest challenges to effectively dealing with and solving a problem or engaging in effective planning is to 'accurately' define the objective or description of your goal or problem at hand. Defining it makes solving it easier.

Knowing your starting point directly impacts your ability to set a course of action to successfully make changes. To uncover the real problem or situation you may need to play detective.

I remember **Peter Falk** playing the 'seemingly' inept detective Frank Columbo, asking questions that didn't, on the surface, have any meaning or relevance to the case. Then suddenly, his method started bringing dramatic results in exposing the culprit. If you can creatively play this role in the beginning to define the objective or real problem, you will set the foundation for success in achieving your goal or resolving your problem.

Jot down your problem or a situation you'd like to resolve. Or, write down a goal that you'd like to achieve. Try to be as clear as and concise as possible.

Problem or Goal:

Now let's put on our sleuthing hats. Use the **6 W's** they taught us in school. **Who, What, Why, Where, When, and How.**

Who?

Who is involved?

Who else needs to be involved?

Who is creating, adding to, or causing this problem?

Who might have a hidden agenda?

Who isn't aware that we have a problem?

Who isn't cooperating?

Who can I count on to help?

Who needs to be involved in making it successful?

What?

What is making this happen?

What needs to happen to make it successful?

What needs to happen to make it go away?

What is different from other results?

What is different from other times we'd done this?

What effect will this decision have on others?

What doesn't work?

What needs to work?

What would be the best possible result?

Why?

Why is this happening?

Why didn't I notice it?

Why wasn't I prepared for this?

Why would I want to change it?

Where?

Where is it happening?

Where did the problem happen?

Where is it affecting us the most?

Where is it not happening?

When?

When did it happen?

When does it occur?

When doesn't it happen?

When did we notice it first?

How?

How did it happen?

How do other people handle something like this?

How does it differ from previous results?

How should I handle it?

The more details you consider, the better chance you have of uncovering the root problem or potential solution. Any other questions that spring to mind?

Redefine and re-state the problem or goal based on your recent research and detective work. This is where you fine tune or refocus your creative energies as you close in on a solution.

Solutions and alternatives: *(List the full range of potential solutions and alternatives for evaluation.)*

Evaluate the pros and cons of each potential solution.

- Do you have the resources?
- Do you have the buy-in needed?
- What would make it work?
- What would stop it?

Which one will you champion or recommend for implementation? Why?

Actions and time lines required to make your best choice solution work.

The important creative questions in the sales process

Ask yourself: Why would this prospect (client) be interested in buying my products or services? Or, dealing with me?

Ask yourself: Have I done my homework?

Ask the Client: What is the most critical issue or concern you'd like to resolve about _____?

Follow up: What makes you say that? What else causes you concern?

Ask the Client: Are you ready to get started? May we have your business?

Ask the Client: Who else do you know that would have a need for my products or services? May I use your name?

Ask the Client: How have we been doing? Are there any adjustments we need to make to better serve you and provide for your needs?

You might wonder why I included this 'sales' piece in a book about creativity. The sales process is all about creativity; creating profitable opportunities to better serve your clients. If you don't investigate their needs and desires, how will you find out where you can be of benefit to them? Asking for help and involving them in the process will build your career.

The foundation for creativity (in sales) is built by asking probing questions and then using those answers in working in partnership with your clients to create the solution they need.

"Every person within an organization represents a hidden reservoir of potential. We never know where the ideas will come from."

Joyce Wycoff, *in 'Transformation Thinking'*

Editor's note: According to a recent **Cap Gemini** *global survey of 260 innovation executives, 43% said their companies have a formally accountable innovation executive (CIO - Chief Innovation Officer), up from 33% the previous year. "Companies with highly aligned innovation strategies and cultures generate 30% higher enterprise value growth and 17% higher profit growth than industry peers," as reported in a recent* **Booz & Company** *study. Hmmm!* **Who is in charge of leading innovation at your organization?**

Ask a question… expect the answer

Ever watch the TV game show **Jeopardy** where contestants try to win by asking questions in light of an answer? Sometimes the secret to solving your problem, to seeing your creativity unlocked, is asking the 'right' questions.

Sometimes, the simple process of 'reframing' your problem or goal as a question can work wonders. Your mind is a wonderful tool, which we too often misjudge and underestimate. Don't be afraid to give it the *stress* test by working it.

Try this technique to unlock the creative powers of your mind in relation to reaching your goal or unlocking the solution to your problem. You can even forget it and sleep on it.

If you frame your objective in the form of a question (**?**) and then let your mind play with it, you may just get the answer you need when you least expect it.

Ask a question - get an answer!

Do your homework and necessary research to break down your problem or expand on your idea. This will provide your subconscious mind with the necessary building blocks or materials to create your answer. Then let it go and sleep on it, if necessary.

Let your inner genius and **Creative S.O.U.L.** work on it.

The answer will come!

Objective	Question
• _____	_____
• _____	_____
• _____	_____
• _____	_____

Break-out-of-the-box Thinking

This creative exercise will 'jog' your problem-solving skills. You can create novel ideas by **NOT** following expectations, rules, regulations, assumptions, or long-standing traditions or company history or policy. Strategically **go against the grain and the status quo** to find the ultimate solution you need.

Just for a moment, **remove the speed limits from your mind** and challenge your traditional linear thinking. Ask yourself these questions to trigger your creative juices.

Look at your problem or idea and ask yourself questions. This will allow you to change the way you look at them. A creative change in perspective can productively change your results.

Take a moment and ask yourself:

- What if?

- If only?

- Why not?

- Who says?

- Does it apply to me?

- By whose standards?

- Is there another way?

- Let's pretend for a minute we had all the resources, personnel, and time.

- Is there a 'second' right answer? A better solution?

- What happens if I do nothing?

- What is the 'best' that can happen?

- What is the 'worst' that can happen?

- How can I benefit or learn from this experience?

These 'mind joggers' will help kick start your thinking and help you look at what you are doing from a new perspective. Take a few minutes and write some answers that relate to your goal or problem at hand. You may find new profitable ways to enhance your career or organization as a result of some honest introspection.

Using this 'contrarian' or non-traditional style of questioning process helps **unlock your creativity**. It is this creativity that holds the seed of your eventual success in reaching your goal or resolution of your problem.

Brain Boosters: (take a minute and play with one or two)

Your job at an advertising agency is to come up with a slogan to promote a new designer white bread. What is it? List 5 famous people you'd hire to be spokesmen for this product and why?

Assume you are blind. Close your eyes reach into a drawer and pick up an object you don't recognize. Describe it using only hearing and touch senses.

Send an email to yourself asking for something of yourself that is legal but something you would '*never*' do. Write a response to yourself explaining why you would <u>never</u> do this.

Five of your friends or colleagues have *secret* middle names. This middle name describes some hidden aspect of who they are. Choose five friends or colleagues and write down that middle name. (*You might tell them if your name and description is complementary.*)

You work with a very noncreative person (a boss or colleague). Think of five things you could do to get this person to be more creative.

"Innovation is not a private act - it is seldom the product of a single individual's intellectual brilliance. Innovation is a product of the connections between individuals and their ideas... It is the constant interplay of ideas, perspectives, experiences, and values that spawns innovation."
Gary Hamel, in 'Leading the Revolution'

Thinking in Reverse to Move Forward

When setting your goals, Steven Covey suggests that we should **"Begin with the end in mind"**.

Would solving this problem be a worthy goal? Focus on the end result or desired result. Take your time and define it carefully. Ask questions that eventually lead you carefully, step by step, back to the current state of affairs or situation. In business it might be called reverse engineering, but it works every time.

Define your ideal solution or desired outcome. Be as accurate as you can.

Ideal Solution:

Keep asking yourself, *"If this is the case, what would have to happen to get this result or stage?"* and use that as your next 'reverse' step. Usually you will find the path within 7 to 12 reverse steps.

Try it, you might just enjoy it!

1. _____ Ideal solution or desired outcome

2. _____ next step (backward)

3. _____next step (backward)

4. _____next step (backward)

5. _____next step

6. _____next step

7. _____present

Use crowd-sourcing to ask for customer input: Snack giant Lay's (division of **Frito Lay**) advertises to ask customers to suggest new potato chip flavors and whole snack categories via its crowd-sourcing website. You could win $50,000 and 1% of sales if your flavor is chosen. **Maple Moose** anyone? Visit **Clorox Connects** and you'll see dozens of ideas shared by Clorox consumers. Tap into the creative genius of your clients to serve them better.

Thunder Thinking... when lightning strikes

"The lightning spark of thought generation in the solitary mind awakens its likeness in another mind." Thomas Carlyle

Is there a way to increase effectiveness and leverage creativity? Is it true that two minds are better than one? Are there advantages to working with others to brainstorm ideas, problems, and dreams?

Thunder thinking occurs when you unleash your mind's creative power and is fully experienced when the lightning of a new idea strikes. But can this creative power be controlled or directed?

From my personal and business experience, I've found that unleashing the creative power of several minds on a single issue can sometimes work miracles. There are many benefits to teaming up for creative problem solving. It can be a lot of fun and bring people closer together, providing a sense of belonging or bonding that enhances relationships and creativity.

Morale can be enhanced when people are solicited for their input and ideas. More good ideas, better ideas, will result if the thunder thinking process is properly used. Frequently communication is improved. Whenever you have more than two individuals involved, team creativity or joint idea-creation can successfully solve problems in family, business, church groups, or community associations.

Webster's defines ***brainstorming*** as "a group problem-solving technique that involves the spontaneous contribution of ideas from all members of the group." This is what I mean by 'Thunder Thinking'.

Alex Osborn, respected author of '*Applied Imagination*', popularized the technique in the late 1930's. Actually, the idea is older than that. I've been told Hindu teachers in India practiced it over 400 years ago.

It works as a part of the creative problem-solving process, occurring during the idea generation or illumination phase. **Thunder Thinking** more accurately focuses this power for productively tapping into your creative genius.

The creative problem-solving guide is a tri-phase process involving ***fact finding***, i.e. gathering information, doing research, and defining the problem. This is followed by the ***idea generation*** phase, as mentioned already.

The final stage or phase is the ***solution selection***, i.e. refining, verification of ideas, and selection of the best possible alternative idea or combination of ideas. Keep in mind that ideas generated during a thunder thinking session need to be evaluated and processed to be productive in their application.

Thunder thinking, as a creative process, provides its greatest benefit in the generation of good ideas, in contrast to our experience in a typical meeting, and in less time too!

The typical committee is normally <u>not</u> a fertile breeding ground for creativity, with participants continually getting bogged down in minutia or in defending their own agenda or viewpoints. I remember a quote that sums it up, *"For God so loved the world that he didn't send a committee."* This is not to down play the valid contribution of committees, but to emphasize their limitations and difference in roles.

Are there rules I should be aware of, you ask? Yes! These will assist you in effective thunder thinking.

Criticism and judgment are suspended, virtually forbidden. Only by suspending judgment do we unleash the power of our individual minds and tap into the real underlying power of SYNERGY. Evaluate later.

Free thinking or wheeling is essential. No idea is too wild, too crazy, or too far-fetched when it comes to attacking the matter at hand. Evaluate later.

Shoot for quantity! Make it your goal to create as many ideas as possible. The greater number *generated* the greater chance of discovering a useful idea.

Work to combine and build on ideas, to improve on them, to add to them as they are mentioned. Encourage participants to value add or layer on the ideas of others as they seek to add new ones of their own.

Work each idea and adaptation until it reaches a natural *pause* and then move on to the next one. In addition, the following **guidelines will help.**

Make the problem to be brainstormed as specific as possible, by breaking it down into its essential components. Focus each participant's energies on a single topic. Accurate problem definition will assist in a solution being generated.

Use thunder thinking for idea finding decisions. Judgment style decisions work better with a balance sheet or pro vs. con approach.

Once you've defined the problem to be brainstormed, **distribute and share the relevant background and parameters with all participants.**

Start each session with a **review and a commitment by all parties to follow the basic rules and guidelines.**

Work to side-step a 'perfectionist' atmosphere. Keep it informal and fun. A spirit of friendly competition could be helpful. Encourage ideas that are stimulated by previous ideas. Get a chain reaction happening. Feed or bounce off each others' creativity and ingenuity.

I find it helpful to appoint one non-participant to act as a recorder, to ensure ideas are captured for future evaluation. This will also ensure participants are not bogged down in the recording process. Focus your individual and group energies on the creative process instead.

Avoid these common thunder-thinking blockers, i.e. phrases that kill the creative process and limit open discussion and idea generation. Be wary if you start hearing them from people on your team, family, or work associates!

1. That is ridiculous!
2. You should have passed on that one.
3. We don't have the time.
4. Pull the other one, it laughs.
5. We did all right without it before.
6. That's not included in our responsibility.
7. Let's form a committee. (*My favorite!*)
8. What will the union (or_____) say?
9. Why change it when it's still working?
10. It's not in the budget.
11. You can't teach an old dog new tricks.
12. That's not practical.
13. That is their problem, not ours.
14. Let's get back to reality.
15. Has anyone else tried it before?
16. We've tried that before.
17. Senior management won't agree to it.
18. This will cost too much!
19. We've never done that before.
20. We're not ready for that.

Add your own. Make sure you don't fall into these negativity traps. Too often, we slip into negative thinking even during a positive, creative period.

Why does it work? Its essential success is within the *chain reaction process.* Essentially idea stimulation occurs in the host brain as well as the participants' brains. The 'associative power' of shared ideas generates a two-way current. When you offer up a new idea, your own imagination - along with everyone else's – is stimulated. *(Just like sharing jokes evokes more jokes.)*

People tend to generate more ideas with other people, in social settings, than they do individually. ***Associative idea generation*** tests have indicated a production increase of over 65% in social sessions compared to solo efforts.

Creative competition can work wonders with mental output increases by up to 50%. The major difference in the concept of **thunder thinking** is in its acceptance of ALL ideas. This specifically rules out the possibility of any 'premature' criticism or judgment stifling the creative problem solving process. Thunder thinking remains effective when all participants learn and agree to follow the **basic rules and guidelines.**

You may be asking, ***"Can I hold thunder thinking or creative problem solving sessions with only two people?"*** Yes, although the more the merrier. Ideally 5-10 people can become an idea generation machine. It can, however, be done with as few as two people. A good partner can stimulate effort in addition to increased associative powers.

There are a few guidelines to keep in mind, which apply to two person creative teams as well as larger creative groups. **They are:**

Ensure there is an incentive for each party. Work to see that values and paybacks are equitable or compatible for each of you if you want to succeed.

Select a specific place and scheduled time to think. Allow time for each of you to rethink the problem. Allow the information to *incubate* in your subconscious brain prior to each meeting.

Get together as planned, to thunder think the problem. Try to **keep it fun and informal.** Bounce ideas off each other. Keep the atmosphere informal and accepting to ensure the idea flow continues. Consider each idea generated. Go for quantity and record them for future evaluation and decision. I've even used a voice recorder, my phone, and/or called home to leave a voice mail to make sure I didn't miss any really good ones.

Take a break; think alone. Review all your joint ideas to date. Do additional research and formulate your ideas. Get back together, **review ideas, and generate new ones.** Start choosing and exploring alternatives found satisfactory to all parties. This is where your judgment, preferences, and personal tastes come into play. This will often result in at least one workable idea.

Remember not to argue! This is the deathblow to the power of creative problem solving. Too many potentially good ideas die on the drawing boards or in the *embryonic* phase when argumentative atmospheres emerge. It's not about right and wrong, it is about generating better solutions.

Intelligent discussion is great! Argument is a dream killer and should be avoided at all costs. As phrased by **Robert Quillen**, *"Discussion is an exchange of knowledge, argument is an exchange of ignorance"*.

We want to work with each other to achieve feats not grasped alone. This goal should allow us to supersede our individual egos to reach better results in our respective lives, careers, and organizations.

Visit: **www.SuccessPublications.ca** to access more publications in our new **Legacy of Leadership series**. They are designed to help equip you and your team to become more productive and profitably grow.

Leveraged technology

Contrary to some thought, technology is not slowing down innovation. It is driving it as entirely new ideas burst into markets that impact how we do business, connect, and even shop.

Denmark based **SuperBrugsen** has a novel idea to ensure the produce they stock appeals to more eco-minded customers. They crowd-source ideas via their website where customers suggest and then staff taste test ideas before they are introduced for sale.

Nike Mexico engages their clients with their Facebook auction, Subasta de Kilometros. Runners earn points for each Kilometer run and can use those to bid on Nike gear.

Brazil based fashion retailer **C&A** leverages Facebook 'likes' on small screens embedded in articles' hangers as generated online. Leveraging real time likes to help fellow shoppers.

A short course in creative decision making

How do you turn around a company with a $285 million loss in fiscal 1997 to post $89 million in profits for the first 6 months of 1998?

- By focusing, teaching and applying the basics of business by making and then implementing decisions that truly served the company and their customers.
- By engaging creative decisions that tackled real problems that were strangling Bay Networks and their staff of 6000.

A 1998 article in Fast Company profiled **David House**. I wanted to share his views and actions that produced this result. Let's review the fundamentals of business and service, as discussed by CEO David House, of Canadian Telecommunications giant Nortel, who led this change in attitudes and results. I've blended in my own thoughts and observations along with his.

"People are hungry for ideas and direction. There are no winners on a losing team and no losers on a winning team," says David House. ***"Our decisions aren't perfect. But, it wasn't important to get things perfect. It was important to get things done."***

And get things done he did! House was able to free up resources and personnel by cutting through the red tape and bureaucracy that had bogged down and overloaded the engineering focus on new products - far too many to support, produce, or ship. This in itself made big changes in the focus and function of the company. Can you do that in your company? Why not?

David House sought to create an 'instant' culture to help focus on the fundamentals of business. *"How do you make decisions? How do you disagree openly? And how do you focus on what's important?"*

David defined culture as, ***"What people fall back on when there are no instructions. It gives you rules for when there are no rules and provides a common language for moving forward."*** Hint: Training your staff provides this culture to fall back on.

To do that David personally created and taught four programs to teach the principles and practices he'd learned in over 22 years at Intel. His courses focused on helping his staff set priorities, allocate resources, and get things done.

He personally taught Bay Network's management team. They were challenged to personally pass on this information by teaching the programs to their 6000 staff. Their results reflected his wise decision to focus on the basics of business - taking care of the customers. His concepts are still valid today.

His **'Decision Making'** course focused on making good decisions - that were informed, timely, aligned with the company's policies and goals and creatively scaled to fit the scope and resources of the company. Do you find yourself bogged down in the decision process when you should be moving into the action process?

His **'Straight Talk'** program provided a direct, timely way to resolve conflict. This could be critical to your ability to get things done by working effectively with your teammates and management. He also did a program on **'Managing for Results'** and another of **'Effective Meetings'**.

Based on my past experience, all of these would prove invaluable to any team or company wanting to effectively use their time or service their clientele. In fact, some of what we do with our clients parallel these. Here are my comments on David's take on 'Decision Making' for your consideration.

Wait until the last minute - but not a minute later

David feels the best decisions are the just-in-time decisions that factor in changing situations and market shifts. But don't use this model as an excuse to not make decisions or procrastinate. Keep doing your homework and keep your research and materials current.

He suggests making the decision as late as possible - but make it in time before you have to take action. There is a fine line between success and missing the wave.

Don't be afraid to argue

"As long as conflict is resolved quickly," says David *"it's good for an organization."* Real leaders deal with conflict head on taking individual feelings seriously, but moving past individual feelings. David suggests one way to effectively move through this process is to agree on *"What the question is."* Agree on the question's wording and make sure it's recorded in writing so everyone can refer to it during the process. Unproductive disagreements often revolve around divergent ideas on 'what is' being decided.

Make the RIGHT decision, not the best decision

"People can spend months debating the 'best' decision," shares David *"without actually arriving at 'any' decision."* Each time you make a decision, you take a risk. But risk is a fundamental part of progress and business survival. **Life is too short.** In every problem or path chosen, 8 out of 10 decisions will work to some degree. Choose the best one and get going.

Disagree - and then commit.

David teaches, *"Not everyone gets a chance to decide, but everyone should have a chance to be heard."* He says the most vigorous debates often yield the most productive, creative thinking. He goes further to state he feels, *"fully supporting decisions that have been properly made is a condition of employment."*

A firm stand and one that bears serious consideration on both parts of the equation: the consultative, creative process of making the decision; and the action process of implementing it by the team. These insightful lessons from David House can have an impact on the way we live and do business. For example:

How we value and effectively use our time and resources both personally and professionally. Being able to effectively focus on the question at hand and move into deciding and implementing a plan of action might spell the difference between success and failure. It might also result in the freedom to fully use our time and create time to spend with the important people in our life.

How we service our clientele and continue to re-position ourselves to meet and exceed their changing needs in an increasingly global market. Being able to make the decisions that affect how we do business and what we offer to our current and prospective clients is the touchstone of business survival and growth.

How we view and tackle the problems and challenges in our respective lives and businesses. In business and life, we face challenges and confront problems and obstacles requiring choices and actions based on those choices.

Being able to cut through the analysis paralysis could be the secret to a fulfilled life and a productive business career. Lessons like these from David House, who faced challenges I hope you and I never face, can be very effective when properly anchored and applied.

I challenge you to digest this information to see where it applies to you, your clients, your company, or association.

- How can you change the ways you and your staff make decisions?

- How can you make changes that affect the way you creatively respond to your clients and their needs?

- How can you make innovative changes that empower and equip your staff to make decisions quickly and fairly on site and in front of your clients?

- How can you make changes to encourage feedback and find out about problems before they become business killers?

- How can you apply this business-based technique to 'real-life' situations or at home?

Perhaps you, like David House, can be the creative 'sparkplug' or energetic leader that leads your team to reinvent themselves and their roles. Perhaps your very existence and profitability depend on your leadership. Perhaps?

A note from Success Publications

We now offer a full series of Leadership Success Packages to assist you in your leadership journey and to enhance your success. They are built around our Legacy of Leadership publication.

- Interested in Leadership
- Engaged in Leadership
- Growing in Leadership
- Committed to Leadership

Visit: www.LegacyofLeadership.ca/Tools.htm to order

We also have a special offer for a 'Leadership in a Box' package for leaders who want to work with their entire teams to equip them to take personal leadership and grow in their roles.

Visit: www.LegacyofLeadership.ca/Box.htm to order

Check out some of our other business and career building publications while you are visiting. We are creating a series of Legacy of Leadership publications. www.SuccessPublications.ca

Let's face it, life is a risk at the best of times. Why not take a calculated one as you move forward in your career or in building your organization? Take care to minimize the potential downside, but be willing to go for it when the opportunity arises.

RISK TAKING

"The people who are playing it totally safe are never going to have either the fun or the reward of the people who decide to take some risk, stick it out, do it differently."
John Akers

"There are risks and costs to a program of action. But they are far less than the long range risks and costs of comfortable inaction."
John F. Kennedy

"Nothing will ever be attempted if all the possible objections must first be overcome."
Samuel Johnson

"You can measure opportunity with the same yardstick that measures the risk involved. They go together."
Earl Nightingale

Take advantage of growth opportunities

At its essence business is based on innovation, solving problems, value-added service; fulfilling the needs, wants, and desires of our clients. Here's a potpourri sampler of how to take advantage of opportunities to build or unlock your business potential by adding to the options, services, and product mix you offer your customers.

What business are you REALLY in? Keep asking this question and keep adapting your business to keep it fresh. Hint: think in terms of customer benefits. What do your clients get when they deal with you? What do they really want? Think **AirBnb** (San Francisco) who are rapidly overtaking top ranked hotels to become the world's top lodging chain.

Combine two or more products or services to create an innovative new one. Perhaps you can work with a strategic partner or ally to develop a new service or product that will bring mutual benefit! Think **Kraft** Dinner!

Take an idea from another industry and transfer it or adapt to suit yours and the needs of your clients. (For example: air miles/coffee cards/buy 10 get one free promotions.) Want to share your car and pick up some extra income? Register it on **RelayRides** or **Sidecar**.

Try something that didn't work the FIRST time. It might now; with changes in technology, resources, client needs, cultures, and attitudes.

Take advantage of the trends or changing interest in the market place. This is where your customer service focus will help, a lot! Think crowd-sourcing!

Use a different material or process to do a traditional job. Creativity counts – actually it can multiply!

Look for ways to be a **value-added** company or person, focusing on real customer service. How can you personally make changes to what you bring to your work?

Being creative is often as simple as being willing to risk by trying new or unfamiliar things and activities. Creativity is what solves your problems and builds your long-term business. Looking at your business with fresh eyes and from different perspectives is one secret in **delivering true value-added customer service.**

Innovate or evaporate – The time to act is NOW!

When would be the best time to start some serious work on innovation in your team and organization to better serve your clients and customers? **Now, is the short answer!** The gap between imagination and achievement or actualization has never been shorter. Beginning 'somewhere' is always preferable to waiting while your team weighs the options and while the organization goes bust or gets left in the dust by those competitors who are being innovative and creative in this volatile market.

Author of *'Leading the Revolution'*, **Gary Hamel** advocates *"Radical innovation is the competitive advantage of the new millennium"*. With the aftermath since 9 - 11, the 2007-08 meltdown; and a general shake up in our economy; Afghanistan, Arab Spring, Iraq, and more recently Crimea, a wake-up call is certainly in order. But that can be a challenge to productive change with some organizations mental constraints and stuck in the mud mindsets. **J.K. Galbraith**, noted economist once shared, *"Faced with the choice of changing one's mind and proving there is no need to – almost everyone gets busy on the proof."*

Everyone needs to be involved. Partial commitment to innovation is a commitment to failure. There needs to be a willingness to listen to and act on the change plan that comes from this innovation process.

Creative Partners' **Andy Radka** shared the results of a survey of 500 top American CEO's. They were asked what their organization needed to survive in the 21st Century.

- Their top answer was *"...to practice creativity and innovation"*.

- However, *"...only 6% of them believed they were tackling this effectively"*.

Quite a gap between stated needs and application. Obviously blending in a spirit of innovation takes time vs. a quick fix or special seminar. If innovation and creativity are so important, even critical in business survival, why the gap in application and implementation?

While each organization is distinct and different, there needs to be a more holistic, integrated approach to innovation and creativity as a culture. We need to get buy in on all levels. Further, we need to consider some important points to increase the possibility of idea generation, which in turn drives innovation and creativity in an organization.

What can you do to facilitate this process within your team? Here are some areas of concern in building a foundation for success under this creative and innovative initiative.

Innovation strategy: Innovation needs to be an 'integral part' of all strategies and policies in your organization, not just 'tacked' on as a quick fix up. It needs to permeate every department and every section. Every employee must make it a focus in part as they do their respective roles. For example, how much time is spent in the boardroom discussing ongoing innovation strategy? This is where the 'rubber hits the road' and your employees see just how much you are committed to this path of action.

Support from top management: In too many organizations, ideas and innovation steps are already at risk at their inception. Poor leadership can look the other way **or** take the courageous step and stretch out a helping hand to buoy them until they can be worked out and tried in the real world.

Ask yourself, *"Do my managers see themselves as leaders whose role is to '**clear the way**' for creativity or are they simply status quo oriented?"* Your employees and colleagues are watching for your leadership in this arena.

What will your employees see when they 'observe' your leadership?

Collective mindsets: Whether we acknowledge it or not we each have mindsets comprised of beliefs, attitudes, and values that drive or motivate our behaviour and applied creativity.

These collective mindsets (e.g. 'can't teach old dogs new tricks' or 'my people aren't creative') frequently form barriers to the creative process. They need to be unblocked and unlocked.

Business guru **Peter Drucker** once said, *"...defending yesterday – i.e., not innovating – is far more risky than making tomorrow."* Make sure your organizational mindset is not creating an 'immune system' or anti-virus system that automatically rejects or attacks new ideas, processes, or challenges to the status quo business model. This can be your largest obstacle in embedding creative approaches and applied innovation within your organization.

Employees get tools and training: Are your staff given the tools and the on-going training they need to support a creative climate and innovation? People and training are crucial to your success and the training needs to be ongoing and reinforced.

Creativity will not magically flourish with the advent of a few courses or the provision of a 'few' creative tools to a 'few select' people. Everyone needs to be trained and supported in his or her evolution of understanding and applied learning.

Knowledge management tools: Does your organization have an intranet that capitalizes on the strides information technology has brought to the battle for business survival?

I.T. (information technology) often acts as an enabler, which allows us to break the traditional barriers of function, geography, and even hierarchy. This allows for internet-based sparking of ideas and a chance to engage and bring 'all' the minds or your various teams into the game. This is how you win! *For example: A few years back, the Titleist (golf company) used 5 of my articles on a new intranet site being set up for their sales staff across the USA.* ☺

What gets measured gets done – apply metrics for innovation: Creativity and innovation can be measured and, if so, are done on a more consistent basis. If creativity is rewarded, even more! Intellectual assets can impact heavily on your market value. Consider the differential and costs between hardware and software values.

Creation of an idea pipeline: Is there an effective innovation process or pipeline or some form of tracking system for converting ideas into innovative services or new products? Is everyone on your team committed to feeding this process or pipeline? Only systematic processes, which incorporate a blend of logical and lateral thinking tools, can bring creativity and innovation. What are you doing to ensure you 'prime the pump' and keep this pipeline full and flowing?

Supplier and customer mindsets: Organizations create a demand for innovative suppliers to be able to serve their clients who are demanding innovative products and services.

Ask yourself, *"Are my current (and potential) clients able to support a dialogue about inventing our shared future?"* How about your suppliers and allied professionals? They may not even recognize the future until they see it or are made aware of its possibilities. That, in part, is your job in the connection and education process of business.

The time to act is now! Innovate or evaporate in the dust of those competitors who saw the need, made the investment, and took the lead. It's your choice!

Your 'Next' Million Dollar Idea

"Empty pockets never held anyone back. Only empty heads and empty hearts can do that!" Norman Vincent Peale

The greatest ideas have been lost to mankind because the minds that spawned them did not capture them or act to bring them into reality. My challenge for you is to **'train your brain'** to systematically look for opportunities to unleash your creative side and bring ideas and innovation into your careers and organizations.

Here are *'classic'* examples of people who were observant and who acted on what they saw, to bring an innovative product or service to life.

- Leo Gerstenzang thought up **Q-tips** when he saw his wife trying to clean their baby's ears with toothpicks and cotton.
- Charles Schneider was fuming at the burnt toast in the factory where he worked – and thought up the **automatic toaster**.
- Mary Phelps Jacob used two lace handkerchiefs and a pink ribbon to create the **first bra** in 1914
- Betty Nesmith noticed she made more mistakes with the newer electric typewriters in 1951. She invented a mixture of water-based paint and a colouring agent to help fix it. She sold her **Liquid Paper** Corporation to Gillette for $47.5 million in 1979
- The 'Next' Million Dollar Idea might just be yours to create…

However, not every idea will be a million dollar one. Nor will every idea will be a major innovative change for your organization. Not every idea will work or pay off when put into practice. But, you will never know until you choose to build foundations for success under the idea and start applying it or at least testing its effectiveness. **The secret is evaluating and then acting on them!**

Committing to creating or capturing an *'idea-a-week'*, will condition and discipline your mind to be on the outlook for opportunities to improve how and what you do, and to add to your product or service mix. These little steps can bring steady growth, income, and success in any industry. **Sometimes, just sometimes, they can bring huge success, fame, and fortune too!**

"Today, creativity must go beyond mere idea generation; the light bulb that goes on over the head of the talented person. It must become an ongoing process, not just momentary and isolated epiphanies…

Creativity, is also a process that is linked to how knowledge is managed, because it is inherently defined by quantum leaps in understanding that lead to the realization of value." **John Kao**

Have you ever seen something and thought, *"Hey, I thought of that first?"* Then, mentally kicked yourself because you never did anything about it? Welcome to the **'I Missed a Million Dollar Idea Club'**.

My first million-dollar idea was 'still-born' in 1970. I was working in youth ministry in Seattle, WA. One day while sitting around with another Canadian, I came up with the idea of a drive through oil change business vs. making an appointment at a dealer. I even went so far as to draft up a simple floor plan adapting an old garage; similar to what I now see when I get my car serviced. I then went on to what I was doing and promptly forgot about it. My friend went home and actually did something with the idea, one of the first of its kind, which grew into a large chain across Canada. Now, every time I drive in to get my oil changed, I am reminded that taking action on our ideas makes them profitable – Ideas At Work!

Why do we do this? Is there a cure to help us? Can we move out of this club and into the **'I acted on my Million Dollar Idea Club'**? The answer is yes! Using a very simple format, I want to challenge you to 'create' or capture an 'idea-a-week' to help enhance your performance, career, or organization.

Commit to analyzing or evaluating each one and then build concrete foundations for success under them. You may not always be able to implement them immediately. You might need some additional training, staffing, financing, technology, additional components, or other pieces, before it can be put into action. Use the idea sheet on page 55. By taking the time to capture them, evaluate each one, and then creatively applying the profitable ones, you will be entering the ranks of the innovators who truly make a difference.

Remember, small, 'incremental' improvements (innovation) can lead to larger returns in building your business. Act on the small ideas too! I wish you success in your journey to enhanced performance and profitability, by honing your curiosity and applying your innovative thinking.

"Once a new idea springs into existence, it cannot be un-thought. There is a sense of immortality in a new idea." **Edward De Bono**

Often we miss the **GREAT ideas** because we don't capture them and then do something with them. Similar to what I teach my students and fellow speakers about writing, *"Capture the idea, make the connections. The rest is editing!"*

Here are a few tips on how to have G.R.E.A.T. Ideas!

Generate quantity and then fine tune for quality. If you want to have quality ideas, you must allow yourself to have a large quantity of them first. Some will have value and some will fall by the wayside. Be curious and creative. Ask questions and generate ideas that have some potential value for you, your organization, or your customers.

Record and capture their essence. Don't hesitate or wait, write down the basic components, genesis, or essence of the idea now. Often they will die if not captured. Ever had a great idea and then later couldn't remember it? Get the bare bones on paper and flesh them out later.

Evaluate potential and costs. After fine-tuning, take a moment to evaluate the idea's potential to enhance your career or business. Calculate the costs to implement it and compare that with the potential earnings or savings. Don't be afraid to challenge your ideas. The GREAT ones will stand the heat and emerge even more valuable. Sometimes you come up with a better adaptation or application of the idea during this process.

Act on it! Here is the key-pivot point to turning potential into profit and performance. Too many great ideas died because they were starved to death by inaction or lack of commitment and follow through.

Track progress and adjust accordingly. Implementation of a great idea, even a million-dollar one, takes time and does not always go smoothly. Factor in time to monitor its progress, make changes in its direction or application, or pull the plug if it isn't panning out as you had envisioned.

Following this simple format will allow you to apply your creative and innovative mind to more productive thoughts and profitable action. Ideas that could be your 'NEXT' Million-Dollar idea'. An 'idea-a-week' could be the turning point in your long-term success and profitability. Make this week the beginning of the most productive year in your life and history.

Brain boosters: (invest a minute to play with these)

A new computer has been developed that can accurately answer any question. What three questions would you ask it?

You are a genetic engineer creating a new species of fish, using the best features of mammals. Describe your fish. Give it a name.

Mental Vitamins and Brain Exercises

The mind works best when challenged with a daily routine of creative thinking. Just as an exercise program is designed to tone and condition the body's muscles, so is exercising your mind helpful.

The late **Earl Nightingale**, noted 20th century self-help expert, devised a very **'simple method'** that **only required three things**:

- An open mind.
- A pencil or pen.
- A pad of paper or something to capture your thoughts and write on.

Here is the system or method he devised. It works as well today as it did when he originally introduced it to his readers and listeners.

Give your subconscious a pressing problem to digest and gnaw on just before you go to sleep. Spend 20-30 minutes thinking about a challenge, problem, or opportunity you are currently dealing with. When you lie down, forget about it. While you sleep your subconscious mind, the source of most breakthrough ideas, will be mulling it over and thinking about it from various perspectives and sides.

Wake up an hour before anyone else. Find a comfortable place to sit, get a coffee or juice, a pad of paper, and a pencil or pen.

Relax and let the ideas flow. Write everything down as the ideas occur, no matter how wild, far out, or seemingly impractical they seem. Don't stop to edit or judge these ideas, just capture or record them. Let your mind do a 'mental dump' onto paper into a form you can do something with later.

This simple solo brainstorming method worked like a charm for Earl, on a regular basis; and produced some outstanding business and recording ideas, which he later launched successfully.

According to Earl the key is the subconscious mind which acts like a gigantic warehouse for ideas and thoughts, floating around just below our conscious mind awareness.

Insights or hunches are ideas, which simply bubbled up from the vast reservoir of our subconscious mind. In essence, while you are studying or feeding your mind a problem or outlining an opportunity (*just before you go to sleep*) is like stuffing your subconscious mind. This feeds your powerful brain new fresh material to play with and from which to work. Try this simple form of personal brainstorming… you might inspire yourself with the wisdom you draw from your own subconscious mind.

Innovation is what you 'DO' with the idea – Ideas At Work!

"…companies are getting better and better at generating new ideas… The processes and capabilities to turn those ideas into reality have become both a constraint and a competitive differentiator. The good news is we are seeing a convergence and a sophistication of thoughts, approaches, and practices that help front-end innovations successfully make it through to the back-end — to implementation. The daunting news is that the challenges and barriers that still stand in the way are equally sophisticated, but long-standing issues. What makes them so difficult to overcome is that they are the human issues. **Here are some examples:**

Existing hierarchical organizations are rarely nimble enough to speedily innovate. Plus, they are rarely able to both deliver against the demands of today AND think about the opportunities of tomorrow.

- Innovation is enabled by and depends upon the connection of strategy, process, structure, and capability.
- Execution is the multiplier of innovation — meaning that an organization that can execute well on a few good innovations is more powerful than one that has lots of great ideas with no way to execute.
- Growing complexity, accelerating pace, and increasing demands are creating a capacity issue for our existing resources — and these resources are the best sources of great ideas.
- Employees want to work on 'stuff that matters'. If you give people some freedom to contribute and think outside their box, they will amaze you.
- Recognition of wins and communicating progress is critically important.
- A critical enabler or significant barrier to an organization's ability to innovate remains its culture.

Just to clarify, we're talking about groundbreaking innovations here — things that cannibalize existing markets, things that disrupt the old models, and services that challenge the embedded ways of thinking and working."

Brief excerpts from remarks shared by Ken Perlman of Kotter International in a Forbes.com article. Included with permission. www.kotterinternational.com/

Ideas At Work! – Priming the creativity pump

Ever notice how some people seem to be more creative, innovative, or just plain 'lucky' at discovering solutions or having ideas strike, just when they need them? Ever wonder how they do it or if they were 'born' that way? Wish you could be more creative? You can!

There is a secret, 'actually a process', which will allow you to access your 'diminished' creative spark and start a flow of good ideas from which the great, innovative, break-through ones might be found. Put simply, you need to **prime the pump** by being aware of what is happening.

I went camping one August; lovely place in Northern Alberta nestled beside a clear, cool lake with lots of trees and natural surroundings. Very rustic and just what I was looking for in my quest to take a mental break from two major writing projects I was working on.

When I say rustic, I mean rustic. No showers, but quaint aromatic out-houses and a fire pit were all that were provided. Water was available by the lake via a pump connected to a well dug 100 plus feet into the ground. It took a lot of pumping, lots of noise, action, and sweat until a rumbling noise was heard coming deep from the earth. Water would gush out. Once flowing, it was easy to maintain the flow while you filled your water container.

Our minds are like that, deeper than we would expect. Often the best ideas are located down in our subconscious, waiting to be pumped to the surface.

Using your mental muscles is like priming the pump, as that is what starts the water or ideas flowing. Being curious about what is happening around you, reading outside your field, asking questions, 'mining' or digging into ideas that interest you – all prime the pump and feed the reservoir from which the break-through, innovative ideas you seek arise. Creativity seems easy and it can be if you are systematic at working your brain. Feed your brain the ideas, the challenges, the opportunities, and lots of facts, background, and other information and see what 'bubbles' to the surface.

But how do you apply this at work? Take a note from some of the other creative people who share in the global market. Perhaps they can teach you something that would be of benefit? A few 'classic' examples to prime your pump.

General Electric under **Jack Welsh**, for example, was famous for 'borrowing' ideas from other sources.

GE was openly researching ideas that could be transferred to their operations and looked at their suppliers, competitors, within their various divisions, and other companies in the market for inspiration. If they saw something that was working, they asked, **"Would this work for us to make us more efficient or more competitive?"** If the answer was 'yes', they would apply it.

According to their own history, GE learned about productivity from Lighting, quick response asset management from Appliances, effectiveness from GE Capital, bullet train cost reduction techniques from Aircraft engines, global accounting management from Accounting. Wal-Mart taught them direct customer feedback – quick market intelligence. They learned new product introduction from Toshiba, Chrysler, HP, Toyota, and Yokagaw. Ford and Xerox shared insights on launching quality initiatives. Hmmm!

What have you learned from your competitors, suppliers, or even your own personnel or departments lately?

Wal-Mart's success was not product specific. **Sam Walton** looked to others for ideas and was able to apply innovation in his various processes for doing business. He used innovation in supplier relationships, distribution, location, and pricing. This allowed him to maintain a competitive advantage in supplying his customers what they wanted, at a price they could afford.

General Motors was the first automobile manufacturer to introduce color to the product mix, which has had some long lasting benefit for that industry and for us as consumers. But did you know they also invented consumer credit, which allowed people who'd never owned a car to be able to purchase one? *(Gee, only 533 more payments and it's finally mine.)*

3M, famous for inventing the Post-it note® (and their champion had to fight to get them introduced as there was no demand at the time, or so the *'experts'* said) has a 30/4 rule in place to encourage its employees to explore new ideas and processes. Simply said, 30% of their sales need to come from products that are less than 4 years old. **Keeps them fresh and keeps them priming the creativity pumps.** What do you do here to keep yourself fresh and primed?

George Westinghouse ran into 'conventional wisdom' when he suggested to a few railroad executives that a train could be stopped by using (air) wind. His imagination was virtually unstoppable. Westinghouse Air Brakes soon became conventional equipment on North American trains and trucks too.

George de Mestral noticed the burrs he was brushing out of his wool pants and his dog's coat. He became curious about the tenacity of the burrs. A little observation under a microscope revealed hundreds of tiny hooks snagged in mats of wool and fur. Years later, he made a connection and the invention of **Velcro ™ fasteners** was born. Einstein would have been proud. *Albert Einstein* on creativity, once said, *"To raise new questions, new possibilities, to regard old problems from a new angle, requires creative imagination."*

Three challenges emerge in priming your creativity pump:

- Think things out fresh; be unconventional
- Destroy the old and then create new.
- Tap into your imagination. Consider new ideas, ask new questions, and raise new possibilities.

Ole Evinrude *was in love and engaged to be married. One summer he rowed his fiancée across the lake to a little island for a romantic afternoon picnic. They had forgotten the dessert. Ole rowed back and returned with the dessert. About midpoint, tired, beat, and sweating under the sun and humidity, he stopped to catch his breath. Although the ice cream was melting, his creative processes were engaged. He said, "There must be an easier way to do this!" This question prompted the invention of the first 'portable' outboard motor in 1906, with a commercially successful version in 1909. Ole got his patent in 1910 and went on to dominate the market for decades.*

Creativity can strike when you least expect it. **Keep priming the creativity pump** and keep your eyes open. You might just surprise yourself and be revealed as a creative leader and rich thinker!

Brain boosters:

Put a ring on a finger on which you don't normally wear a ring. Notice how constant awareness of something so small makes a difference.

Organs and pianos have foot pedals. What if we used foot pedals for computers? What computer functions would you attach to the pedals?

The days of the week are color coded. What colors would you choose?
Monday _____ Tuesday _____ Wednesday _____ Thursday_____
Friday _____ Saturday _____ Sunday _____ and why?

The following pages outline two distinct problem solving styles. We include them for your creative reference.

Creative Problem-Solving

"Today many North American corporations spend a great deal of money and time trying to increase the originality of their employees, hoping thereby to get a competitive edge in the marketplace. But such programs make no difference unless management also learns to recognize the valuable ideas among the many novel ones, and then finds ways of implementing them." **Mihaly Csikszentmihalyi**

Many teams find that a more creative, less rigid approach to solving problems often yields the highest quality solution. However, first each needs to understand what factors make creative thinking work best. Otherwise known as the *'association of ideas'*, creative thinking is the process by which imagination feeds off memory and knowledge to cause one idea to lead to another.

This chapter is designed to help individuals identify what factors are necessary for a productive creative problem-solving session and to provide a process for thinking creatively. It will also give your group an opportunity to apply and practice some creative thinking skills.

IDEA: Pull together some of your more creative team members. Have them read through this chapter and set aside some creative Thunder-Thinking time to help tackle your specific challenges and creative opportunities.

Requirements for Creative Thinking

The key factors that influence team success in any creative thinking session are:

Suspend Judgment

By far the most important characteristic of effective creative problem solving is to have an open mind. Your team should work on creating a supportive environment where judgment and criticism are not permitted. For the process of brainstorming, these qualities stifle creativity.

Self-Assessment

In order to develop a more open mind, it may help to determine your tendency to cling dogmatically to your ideas and opinions.

Develop a Positive Attitude

Have enthusiasm and optimism for your ideas, even if they seem wild and unrealistic. Develop an attitude that all ideas are good ideas, as cynicism will only inhibit creative thinking.

Use Checklists

There are a couple reasons why your team should write down EVERY idea, no matter how far-fetched. First, it sends the message to the team that everyone's ideas are valued and helps create a supportive environment. Second, recording all ideas will ensure that nothing important is forgotten and give the team an opportunity to go back and combine parts of one idea with parts of another, letting ideas feed off each other.

Be Self Confident

Remember that many of the world's greatest ideas were ridiculed at first. **Have faith in your creativity!!!** Some of our most basic scientific principles like that the Earth is round and revolves around the sun never would have been advanced without the confidence and courage to go against the grain.

Encourage Others

Praise and encouragement are the fuel for creativity; it enables ideas to flow freely and motivates team members. Instead of criticizing or rejecting an idea, offer praise and encourage your team to keep up the good work!

The Creative Thinking Process

Below is a summary of the stages of creative thinking. These stages resemble the steps in the reflective approach to problem solving, with adjustments to encourage creativity and exploit brainstorming.

Stages in Creative Problem Solving

Orientation

This step of the creative thinking process is a matter of setting the stage for a productive session, i.e., making sure you have all the necessary requirements for an open and creative group process. If necessary, review the information in the previous topic. In addition, the team should generate a list of topics or headings for which it plans to gather ideas.

Preparation and Analysis

This stage is primarily devoted to **fact-finding**. While gathering facts is important, it is only necessary to gather those facts that will serve to further creative thinking. Getting bogged down in too many details at this stage may actually restrain creative thinking efforts. There will be time later to go back and fill in the facts you need as you go.

Go back to the headings generated in the orientation phase. Are there any headings that don't seem relevant to your task at this time? Focus on gathering facts for those topics that will help you identify causes for the problem you are trying to solve. You might also research successful past solutions to similar problems.

Analyzing the data collected is an important part of helping to reveal clues to the solution. It is primarily geared toward establishing relationships among the facts you have collected.

Look for similarities, differences, and causes by asking questions like *"What does this fact have in common with that fact?"* or *"How are these things different?"* and *"What would cause this effect?"* Analyzing data in this way will help you develop a framework for generating solutions.

One final note about fact-finding is to be sensitive to the 'distinction' between those topics that can and will require an immediate decision and those that will require additional 'creative' thinking and financing.

For example, if cost is a concern to your team, find out exactly how much money is available for your task. This is a decision that must be made in light of available resources, whereas developing a solution that fits within your budgetary constraints will require creative thinking.

Brainstorming

The philosophy behind brainstorming is that the more ideas there are on the table, the more likely a suitable solution will emerge. This stage of the process is a 'freewheeling' exchange of ideas to get together a list of as many possibilities as you can.

Remember to write down all ideas, no matter how far-fetched they may seem, and to maintain an open mind at all times. Let ideas feed off one another and feel free to combine parts of one solution with another or alter ideas in various ways.

Incubation

Incubation is the 'time-out' stage of the process in which group members disperse for a period of time to let ideas grow and to encourage 'illumination' of the correct solution. While a time-out may not always be practical for every problem-solving team, it is nonetheless considered an important part of the creative process so as not to let creativity lag by overworking the mind.

Whether the time-out is a lunch-break, a good night's sleep, or a week's hiatus before the next meeting, the purpose should be not to force the mind to think about any particular aspect of the problem or solution.

It should however, be time-out to let the mind 'meander' as it wants. Some of the world's most creative people rely on these moments of silence and solitude for their best ideas. If it is at all possible for the team to take a break from its task, incubation should be incorporated into its activities. In my case I went so far as to buy a 'creative place' out in the country 45 minutes northeast of Edmonton, Alberta. The creative challenge and lack of interruptions have been invaluable over the last fourteen years. We now live here full time and I continue my creative approach to semi-retirement. This book is one of them.

Synthesis and Verification

Out of all the possibilities the team has generated during its brainstorming session, the ideal solution should be a combination of the best qualities of each idea. During the orientation and analysis phases of the process the team's job was to break apart the problem, the task at hand now is to 'construct a whole' out of the ideas and fragments generated by brainstorming.

One good way to do this is to make a list of all the desirable qualities or disadvantages that a solution might have and then rate each idea generated. Each quality or disadvantage can be weighted in terms of its importance or applied without weighting. The idea with the best overall profile can then be identified.

A second way of **synthesizing** ideas is to create an outline or grouping of ideas, with similar ideas assigned to the same group and relations between groups of ideas mapped out.

Verification is the final phase of the process and requires testing the solution the team has chosen to see if it achieves all the team's goals. I trust you find some of these ideas of value in your quest to tap into your creative power and unleash your inner genius.

Reflective Problem Solving

No decision-making team follows exactly the same procedure for solving problems as another team. Regardless of how you and your team members approach a problem, however, most high-quality decisions are reached by performing certain functions.

Reflective problem-solving emphasizes the importance of **basic tasks: defining concepts, identifying needs, and identifying and evaluating solutions.** Groups using reflective problem solving make sure to cover an agenda of these key tasks, usually in a standard order. This section will give you a brief checklist of tasks and suggestions about how to organize discussion effectively to address them.

Problem Solving Tasks

From this perspective, **there are five key points involved in problem solving**:

1. **Define the problem**: Make a list of resources - people, books, web sites, etc. - that have some connection to and information about the problem you are trying to solve. Use these resources to clarify any unfamiliar terms or concepts and to clarify for the group what you understand the problem to be.

At this point you are **looking for symptoms, evidence that a problem exists, not causes,** which in the next step will explain *why* a problem exists.

2. **Analyze the problem**: After the group has discussed the evidence for the existence of the problem and defined what that problem is, you can now turn your attention to analyzing the evidence more thoroughly, **looking for relevant data** that may explain why the problem exists. This step in the procedure is a matter of evaluating the data you've collected and the sources it comes from.

3. **Establish criteria for evaluating solutions**: Set an objective with your group that all proposed solutions should strive for. Based on your definition of the problem and analysis of its cause(s), this objective should be the **one specific goal that any acceptable solution should attain**.

If the problem you are trying to solve is too complex to set only one objective, another means for establishing criteria to evaluate proposed solutions is to make a list of MUSTS and WANTS.

Often the best way to create a breakthrough in your problem solving is to break down your challenge into smaller more manageable pieces. Then solve it in sections.

MUSTS are those basic requirements without which the solution would be unacceptable (deal breakers, if you will).

WANTS are those qualities that are 'desirable' in any solution and should be prioritized from most desirable to least desirable. This type of checklist may help your group maximize the effectiveness of any solution without omitting any essential requirements.

4. **Propose solutions**: After you have established some basis for evaluating solutions, try brainstorming solutions. From the list of solutions that emerge from your brainstorming session, develop a realistic range of solutions and select the one that best fits your needs according to your evaluation criteria.

5. **Take action**: Write an action plan that details the steps that need to be taken in order to implement your solution and the resources needed to do it. The manner in which your group performs these necessary problem-solving tasks is incidental, so long as you address each function. However, some groups find it helpful to follow a more detailed and systematic process for problem-solving to help keep them focused. If you and your team members are having difficulty staying on track, following this step-by-step process - keeping in mind the essential tasks outlined above may help you reach your goal more efficiently and effectively.

Organizing Discussion

Problem solving groups tend to encounter a set of common trouble areas. The following attitudes and strategies will help your team can avoid these trouble areas.

Avoid focusing TOO much attention on premature solutions. Refrain from acting on the 'first' suggestion of a solution before the problem has been thoroughly defined, its causes discussed, and a range of solutions evaluated. Don't fall for the **'first right'** answer trap. Go for the best answer!

Don't avoid problems. Many people dodge problem-solving activities because they have a low tolerance for uncertainty. This can lead to a 'quick-fix' attitude that seeks to eliminate the problem as quickly as possible by whatever means necessary. Work on cultivating endurance for ambiguity and doubt and become actively involved in the entire problem-solving process.

Refrain from dogmatism and becoming fixated on specific ideas. At all times maintain an open mind and be willing to consider new problems and new ideas.

Be careful of your own biases and the biases of other sources when evaluating the facts of a case. The challenge is objective investigation and judgment.

Don't make sweeping generalizations of accepted facts or beliefs without sufficient evidence that comes from reliable sources.

Don't misinterpret honest disagreement for dislike. Recognize that group members all have different backgrounds, values, experiences, and thinking styles that have significant bearing on how an individual views a problem.

When someone expresses a different opinion or disagrees with you, don't take it as a personal attack. View this difference in opinion as a positive consequence of the group's diversity that will help everyone think through the problem more carefully. Different opinions and viewpoints bring a healthy perspective and a better chance of a more impactful solution. They are really an indication of a creative, healthy team!

More thoughts on Unlocking Your 'Business' Potential

When all is said and done, there are essentially three ways to increase your business.

- Work to increase the **number of clients** you attract to visit and retain to deal with you.
- Work to increase the average **size of the sale** for each client.
- Work to increase the frequency or **number of times** each client returns and buys again.

Look for ways to **attract more clients** in the services and product mix you offer. Kind of like the comparison of having a single line in the water vs. having multiple lines with different baits. Which one will have the best chance of catching more fish? What kind of bait do you have?

How about looking for ways to **add-on or cross sell?** Adding-on helps move the client to a larger or superior product, package, or service.

Adding-on is based on really understanding the intended use and realizing the basic product or service will fail to meet the real needs of your client.

Cross selling introduces your client to additional products or service. Offer them alternatives that perform better and are in their best interest. Phone providers do this well with bundling options: Voice mail, call waiting, auto call back, 2nd line, autodial, caller ID, 3rd line for security,4th line for fax, cable and computer information delivery systems. Whew! More recently TV too!

Test your offerings, product mix, and services offered. Experiment with your Web site, advertising, promotional materials, sales and direct mail letters, live sales presentations and in store demos, guarantees, USP's, pricing points, volume purchase and discounts, or financing. See what works! Keep refining until you find something that is effective and then update it as needed to keep it fresh and relevant to the changing market place and client needs.

Look for ways to form **strategic alliances** with those companies who are already dealing with the people you would like to attract; companies who have already earned their trust and respect. If you offer complimentary, non-competitive services or products that assist them in serving their clients you will find a more favorable response. Look for opportunities to offer this kind of connection to people who want to deal with your clients and who offer something you don't offer or are unable to do so profitably at this moment.

Condition your mind to look for break through ideas and creative solutions. Investigate other industries, look at their success stories and best practices and see if they hold a secret that you can transfer to yours. For example: Fed-Ex simply built on the idea of the central distribution system used by the banking system for its courier delivery. **Fred Smith** did ok with this transplanted break-through!

As my friend and fellow author **Jay Abraham** who taught me some of this, says, *"Break throughs let you out think, out leverage, out market, out sell, out impact, out defend, out maneuver, and continuously outwit your competition at every level."*

Look for **breakthrough/transferable ideas** in marketing, innovation, creativity, operations, sourcing, technology, systems, process, selling, financing, product mix, service list, and distribution. Learn from competitors as well as people operating in non-related industries and market segments. This can be a valuable investment of your time and research.

Creating a Master Mind Alliance or Success Team

What is 'your' dream?

- To own a new home?
- To start a new business? A new career?
- To impact your community?
- To travel the world?
- To write a best selling book (or 3+) or to become a professional speaker?
- To build a profitable business that is a model of value-added customer service in your community?

If you've encountered a few detours enroute to your dream, experienced frustration or bouts with indecision, **I'd suggest a helpful approach.**

Mastermind Alliances or Success Teams can play a pivotal role in ensuring your dream becomes a reality. I proved this to myself 20 years ago in my quest to become a more productive speaker and successfully enter a new arena.

- How does a relative newcomer to Toastmasters International find himself speaking at the world-class level with more experienced professional speakers in their professional level Accredited Speaker Program?
- How do three Vancouver area speakers audition, defy the odds, and earn the opportunity to speak on the world stage?

This incredible saga began with an exploratory Mastermind/Success Team meeting in April 1994, when seven of us discussed our common goal of entering the Accredited Speaker Program. A solid commitment from each member to research and work as a team was agreed upon. Then as the work began, members assessed their own experience and qualifications.

In light of a lengthy and onerous judging process, each of us brought our concerns, questions, and fears to our monthly meetings. With mutual support and brutal honesty, each question was answered and basic qualifications double-checked. Qualifying speeches were drafted, practiced, and exhaustively critiqued by fellow team members, prior to recording our live audition tapes.

Each year since 1981, Toastmasters International has invited a handful of qualified speakers to present at their annual international convention in the Accredited Speaker program, **"...*designed to recognize those Toastmasters who have attained a professional level of excellence in public speaking.*"**

To date, (June 2014) only 63 Toastmasters around the world have earned this prestigious A/S award in their 90-year history. Canada claims 7 of these 63 world class speaking professionals. **www.AccreditedSpeakers.com**

In October 1994 three (A.S.K.) **Advanced Speakers Klub** members submitted applications and audition tapes; I was one of them. Of the 32 world-wide who survived the initial screening and 1st level judging process, only five would eventually be invited to San Diego in August 1995. In February 1995 my two fellow team members and I received notification that the judges had voted to advance each of us to the world stage. We would speak in front of a live audience and panel of five judges.

Three for Three! Results that had never occurred in Toastmasters International history. The normal applicant success rate in making the finals is only 20%, and some years no one advances to level two or attains the award.

Can a Mastermind Alliance or Success Team play a vital role in the eventual achievement of your personal or professional goals or in turning dreams into realities? Just ask **Judy Johnson, Margaret Hope**, or myself! Margaret Hope, DTM, A/S became the 41st person in the world to become accredited in 1995. I had the pleasure of being presented with mine (number 48) in 1998 in front of a crowd of over 2000 excited Toastmasters in Palm Desert, California. It works! Visit: www.AccreditedSpeakers.com for information on this program.

- Can a Mastermind Alliance or Success Team really help you in achieving your dreams? YES!
- Can they help build your business and help your staff succeed? YES!
- Can they help to bring your ideas to life? YES!

What are they and how do they work?

Success Teams gained wider recognition in 1979 with the publication of a book entitled *'Wishcraft'* by **Barbara Sher** and **Annie Gottlieb**.

"A SUCCESS TEAM is a small group of people whose only goal is to help every member of the team get what he or she wants."

The concept has been around for centuries. **Napoleon Hill**, author of *'THINK AND GROW RICH'*, (1937) espoused a form of Success Team with his Mastermind principle, *"...whenever two or more minds are blended in a spirit of perfect harmony, for the pursuit of a definite purpose, there is born of that alliance a power which is greater than that of all the individual minds combined."*

Your personal Mastermind Alliance or Success Team may be focused on a specific project or a long-term goal. It may have a fluid format with members joining and leaving as their dreams evolve or a more structured long-term membership. It's up to the individual members. It might be people in your own industry who bond to help each other win or a group of your staff focused on improving your business.

These ingredients will help ensure your Success Team's success

A firm commitment by each member to encourage and assist team members in their personal growth and to achieve their goals.

Regular meetings where goals, challenges, and dreams are shared, progress is reported, and problems are defined and brainstormed. Specific steps are then outlined to enable the members to make solid progress towards their respective dreams.

A positive attitude, encouragement, personal integrity, and confidentiality by each member. A high level of trust must exist if team members are to be open to honest input from fellow team members. This is where the real growth occurs.

One individual will often take the lead to recruit a team of fellow dreamers or achievers. Perhaps, they have observed the secret of synergy, of applied power, through shared purpose and focus, of building on the experience and insight of others.

Choosing your team is a unique learning experience! It helps if members are positive and have desires and some experiences in harmony with your team's needs. If for example, your Success Team has a business orientation, you might recruit members with a variety of specific business experiences along with members who are starting a new business. Don't be afraid to pause periodically and re-assess your group and your individual progress. Make any course corrections necessary to keep your group on track.

*One of my earliest recollections of an effective Mastermind Alliance or Success Team was in college. A group of marketing management students formed a study team to handle the weekly 'killer' assignments. We would each read the required material and meet to brainstorm the assignment, break down the problem, and suggest alternatives and solutions for each problem. Then, we'd retire to write our individual reports. **Our results: We led the class in our understanding of the problem and in generating creative solutions for each assignment.** We also spent less time in the process, as each of us was busy in our respective management careers.*

Mastermind Alliances and Success Teams mirror some characteristics, in shared experience and contacts with networking. However their difference and remarkable effectiveness is solidly built on the principles of ongoing personal honesty and mutual accountability.

They operate on the premise that 'YOUR' group is dedicated to helping 'YOU' achieve your dreams and to keep 'YOUR' commitments, as well as acting as a resource for 'YOUR' success.

I worked even harder to complete my commitments, because I didn't want to let my success team or myself down. There were late evenings before a meeting working on projects. I continued to learn the secret of setting realistic goals, organising my weekly objectives, and pacing myself to reach them.

Define group formats and meeting times early to ensure each member actively participates in a majority of the meetings and receives his or her share of time and assistance. This is essential to the survival, effectiveness, and success of your team.

One of my groups met weekly for a 7AM breakfast. Each member got 15 minutes of the group's focus. We would take the first 2-3 minutes in updating the group on our progress (or lack) during the past week, 7-8 minutes to outline and brainstorm problems, concerns, goals, and objectives with input from group members, with the last few minutes spent outlining specific ACTION steps to be taken during the next week.

This was the group who assisted me as I launched my career in the speaking and training industry. Their insight and support has proven a godsend over the years as I wrote and published my books and travelled North America and other countries sharing my **Ideas At Work!** *with thousands of professionals and expanded my business ventures. I owe them a giant debt for their assistance.*

Another member went on to pen two North American best selling books and now has a lucrative speaking business as well. I've followed her lead.☺ This was a short-term, goal-specific, focused success team. Though the time frame was shorter the results have been amazing over the years.

Each Success Team will take on its own characteristics, as members share their essence, experience, and dreams. Often this will be the highlight or 'power-point' to your week. You bounce ideas and problems off the creative minds of your team, while gaining their support and respect on your progress. Your team becomes a personal coach and cheerleader, to help keep your focus and energy in pursuing your dreams.

Dreams are a powerful part of your personal growth. As you build strong *foundations for success* under each dream, draw on the energy, insight, and strength of your Team and, in turn, give them yours. TOGETHER, you will all succeed!

I believe in the power of success teams, having experienced their support and help over the years. Find other people in your community or industry who are as dedicated to building their careers and businesses as you and start your own. The results will be more than worth your investment.

When I moved to Edmonton in 2000 to 'semi-retire' from my overly-active travels as a professional speaker and trainer, I again formed a Success Team. I pulled together four other speakers who were serious about moving their expertise and business profitably to the next level. Three of us had already established our speaking businesses and two of our team were relatively new to the arena.

We met monthly and shared ideas, resources, and shoulders as needed. In less than a year our 'rookies' had successfully launched their speaking careers and the remaining senior members had seen a marked increase in our business and what we were providing to our respective clients. In addition to our mastermind group meetings and activities we found ourselves doing some *creative* projects and marketing as a team. We also pooled our resources to allow us to invest in additional training and materials we would share.

In 2007, I led a group of speakers to launch **www.AlbertaSpeakers.com** and later several additional regional sites to help us creatively reach and attract clients for our respective businesses. We've expanded that to include other colleagues who have seen the creative power of collaboration. Last year (2013), I led a group of fellow Accredited Speakers who banded together to launch a similar online project. **www.AccreditedSpeakers.com** Both of these joint ventures have been very helpful individually and profitable too.

In 2000, I spent 3 days in Tempe, Arizona along with 65 fellow CAPS and NSA leaders in the Speaking industry, talking and sharing ideas about how we could work together and by combining our efforts achieve the common goals we held. It was worth the time and investment needed to be there. I later returned to serve on the NSA Chapter Leadership Council for two years to assist other emerging leaders at similar gatherings.

So ask yourself:
- **What is it you really want in life?**
- **In business?**
- **What will you change to make it happen?**

Leverage the power of a mastermind or success team and see it become a reality!

2014: And now the rest of the story

Veteran broadcaster **Paul Harvey** was famous for his reports. He was even more famous for the above words and then sharing a little known fact or twist that completed the story. It is only fitting that I update my readers with the rest of the Dream Works story mentioned earlier.

Margaret Hope, DTM, A/S went on to expand her career as a professional speaker, trainer and presentations coach. She is now an adjunct professor at UBC and best-selling author of *'You're Speaking... But Are You Connecting?'* **Judy Johnston, DTM** moved into a new career as a coach and counselor with the Self-Employment Program offered by BC's Douglas College. She has now retired from that role.

On Saturday August 22nd, 1998 standing off stage I was overwhelmed to hear my name being called as Toastmasters International's 48th professional level Accredited Speaker. I walked across that Palm Desert, California stage to the thunderous applause of 2000 plus of my friends and fellow Toastmasters.

The journey to my dream of being a well-paid professional speaker started in 1990 when I asked Past International President **John Noonan, A/S** about the National Speakers Association and was *gently* directed to join Toastmasters. Along the way I learned to respect my abilities and willingness to set goals and to attain them despite of numerous setbacks and disappointments. I challenge you to DREAM BIG! - to ACT on your dreams. **For it is only by acting on our ideas and dreams, along with the help of others we enlist, that we see them built and successfully brought into reality.**

Brain boosters: (take a minute and play with one or two)

Write your name upside down – and backwards! This means you have to start from the last letter in your name. Notice how this feels.

Make up a list of 'socially acceptable' activities people could do while standing in line.

Draw a picture of a nature scene only using triangles.

A new business magazine has just been created, unlike any others on the market thus far. What is the name of this magazine and what is its focus?

Note: I love these ideas to challenge your brain someone sent to me more than a dozen years ago. Wish I could remember who sent them so I could give them credit. They are amazing tools to train your brain.

In the mid 80's I belonged to 'The Entrepreneurs Association'

Our Association Credo was:

"I do not choose to be a common man (or woman). It is my right to be uncommon, if I can.

I seek opportunity, not security! I do not wish to be a kept citizen, humbled and dulled by having the state look after me.

I want to take the calculated risk, to dream and to build, to fail and to succeed. I refuse to barter incentive for a dole. I prefer the challenges of life to the guaranteed existence; the thrill of fulfillment to the stale calm of utopia.

I will not trade freedom for beneficence, nor my dignity for a handout. I will NEVER cower before any master, nor bend to any threat.

It is my heritage to stand erect, proud and unafraid; to think and act for myself, to enjoy the benefit of my creations and to face the world boldly and say, 'This with God's help, I have done.' All this is what it means to be an Entrepreneur."

Entrepreneur Magazine was initially our Association publication.

Theodore Roosevelt, who was often criticized, wrote,

"It is not the critic who counts, not the man who points out how the strong man stumbled, or where the doer of deeds could have done them better. The CREDIT belongs to the man (or woman) who is actually in the arena, who strives valiantly - who knows the great enthusiasm, the great devotion ... and spends himself (or herself) in a worthy cause. Who at best, knows the triumph of high achievement; and at the worst, if he (or she) fails... at least fails while daring greatly, so that his (or her) place shall never be with those cold and timid souls... who know neither victory nor defeat."

If you are to get criticism, and you will, let it be for following your own path and personal leadership; and in daring to set your goals higher and build your dreams.

"Do not follow where the path may lead ... go instead where there is no path and leave a trail", writes another unknown scribe. Take a lesson and a sage tip from me, *"Remember, they don't build monuments to critics."* 'Prepare yourself to WIN!' by applying your creativity to the challenges and opportunities you encounter!

Mistakes... leverage your lessons for success!

"Crisis can often have value because it generates transformation...
I have found that I always learn more from my mistakes than from
my successes. If you aren't making some mistakes, you aren't
taking enough chances." John Sculley

Like many of you, I hate making mistakes; and worse yet having to admit them and clean up after them. Earlier in life, this was an area of challenge for me in my growth as a person and in establishing my business. But, I am learning and building on the lessons. That is the most important thing.

Someone once told me, *"Learn from the mistakes of others, you'll never live long enough to make enough of your own"*. At the time, that sounded ludicrous to me. I didn't want to admit my own, let alone discuss them with someone else or hear about theirs. As I reached a more 'seasoned' milestone birthday (April 2014) I looked back and see the wisdom in this advice. I now build on their lessons with my clients.

About ten years back I read an article, while flying to a speaking engagement in the USA, about a company who had tackled this 'mistake-itis' full-on, and had turned it into a **value-added training tool** for their company.

What they did was invite their management and staff to submit their mistakes and each month they voted on the biggest mistake and gave a decent cash prize for the 'winner'. **Initially I thought, *"What a dumb idea!"***

But, as I finished reading the article, I began to see the wisdom in their process. What they had discovered was needless 'repetition' of mistakes throughout the company were costing them valuable manpower and additional resources. Someone would make a mistake, quietly fix it, and simply continue without talking about it. In fact, the corporate climate was such that mistakes were not openly discussed.

Then someone else would repeat the mistake. The costly cycle would continue unabated as people continued to waste time, resources, and money doing the same 'wrong' things. The positive results of developing a culture where mistakes were accepted as a normal part of doing the work and making progress proved to be amazing. Their company-wide commitment to 'openly' **sharing these mistakes and the resultant lessons learned was the key point to their success and growth.**

- Sharing the mistakes and the lessons gleaned from those mistakes leveraged the learning curve of their management and their staff.
- It allowed them to side-step or avoid needless repetition of mistakes and all of the lost time and costly resources that repetition entailed.
- This freed up much needed resources and finances for other ventures.
- It allowed the company to grow and expand on a stronger foundation.
- It encouraged its management and staff to be more open to innovation and to take educated risks in developing new business, services, and products to better serve their changing clientele.

Food for thought

- What was your most recent mistake?
- What did you learn from it?
- Have you shared the lesson you learned with your team?
- Do you have a corporate climate that realizes mistakes are a part of the innovation process and celebrates the lessons enroute to success?

One of my biggest lessons in life was learning how to 'recycle' my mistakes; to learn from each one, savor the lesson, and move ahead boldly to make some new mistakes. Plus, make some new progress from that process!

"You know, by the time you reach my age, you've made plenty of mistakes and if you've lived your life properly, so you learn. You put things in perspective. You pull your energies together. You change. You go forward." Ronald Reagan, former US President

Interestingly enough, in my role as a speaker and consultant I am now able to draw from the lessons from my past 'mistakes' and **not only do my audiences and clients profit from them – so do I!**

Brain boosters:

Imagine you are from another planet. You go back to your home planet and attempt to explain why men on earth wear ties.

Think of five new names for clouds. Describe what kinds of clouds they are.

Look around you right now. Name as many things as you can in the next two or three minutes that begin with the letter 'B', or 'G'.

Food for thought...

"Management is doing things right;
Leadership is doing the right things!"
Peter Drucker

"Companies fail to create the future, not
because they fail to predict it but because
they fail to imagine it."
Gary Hamel, in 'Leading the Revolution'

"Someone once told me that my ability to
earn a 'substantial' living would be directly
dependent on my ability to solve problems
- to help people make decisions."

"Effectiveness - often survival -
does not depend on how much effort we
expend, but on whether or not the
effort we invest is in the right direction."

Bob 'Idea Man' Hooey
Creative Catalyst and Idea Farmer

By now you've realized we have 'seeded' this book with numerous questions, brain boosters, and other ideas to challenge and train your brain. This is where you tap into your creative genius. We all have one, but many of us have let it atrophy from lack of use. We challenge you to enhance your creative muscle.

Fuel your creativity

"An idea is a feat of association." Robert Frost

One of the fun activities I use to keep myself fresh and creative is to allow myself to engage my mind with a free flow of ideas. Often creative or innovation nuggets will come from spending time thinking about diverse things from a different perspective.

Here are some random tips, thoughts, and quotes for your reflective consideration. Please allow you mind to wrap around a few of these new thoughts. Unlock your creativity - let your mind soar! *"Imagination is more important than knowledge,"* according to **Albert Einstein**.

The most innovative ideas quite often started with 'seemingly' ridiculous thoughts. The more ridiculous, unusual, or abstract your idea, the better likelihood of it containing the 'seed' of a remarkably innovative solution to your problem. You know you're an old dog when you stop learning new tricks. Remain teachable to be more creative! I teach some of these in person.

Warm up your creativity. Just for fun take two unrelated objects and quickly imagine as many comparisons or connections between them as possible. For example: an elephant and a diamond. Both have different facets, both come in different sizes and colors, and both come from Africa.

Practice mental pinball to build your associative skills. Strong creative thinkers let their thoughts skip, jump, and dart like the activity in a pinball machine. They let their thoughts bounce off ideas and take quantum leaps in a multitude of directions. Take one word or thought and see if you can freely associated 20 items or thoughts. Reach 20, stretch your mind and go for 30.

Creativity in looking at other areas, worlds, or industries can spark the solution you need. For example: In creating customer loyalty or increased usage you might look at what the airlines are doing with frequent flier miles. Ask yourself what can I do like the frequent flyer programs to increase usage in my business? The ideas might just amaze you and be simple to implement.

Do you have a **creative environment** that brings out your best thinking? Create an environment that is conducive to creative thought; e.g. casual clothes, warm room (not too warm), soft couch, fireplace, soft music, walking outdoors on a lovely day, working in a darkened room, etc.

Just like athletes who go through rituals to help themselves psychologically feel and play better, you can create one that works, for you. Give this some thought and then **ACT!**

What would a famous person do? Challenge yourself to think how a few distinctly different celebrities or historical figures might approach your problem. How would the Pope, Mother Theresa, Steve Jobs, or comedian Jimmy Fallon tackle the problem? Use the trigger points generated by what you think they would do, as the tools to find the ideas to help you solve it.

TEAM THINK: Meet weekly with a 3-5 person team for the specific focus of brainstorming solutions to each other's problems. Change at least one person on the team periodically to help keep the perspectives fresh, the creative energy levels high, and the ideas flowing.

Think Positive - if you want to think creative. Idea killers like, *"We've tried that before."* or *"That's a dumb idea!"* will damper the creative juices and flow and quickly extinguish the creative flame. Why not ask yourself, *"How can we build or improve on that?"* or *"Let's look at the workable parts of that idea and see where it will lead us!"* Your perspective can be the key that unlocks any problem.

Go for quantity if you want quality. Generate as many ideas as possible - good ones, bad ones, fuzzy ones, even stupid ones - to find the really high pay-off and usable ones. Just like you take a multitude of photographs to get enough shots to be able to pick a good one; why not do the same with your idea machine (brain).

Solutions come when least expected - and when they are not forced. While ideas come like love at first sight, those gushers are the exception. Trying to force an idea is similar to trying to force love between two people, usually gives the same results. Ideas come in the shower, while walking, or while day dreaming.

Team Works: Trying to solve a tough problem by yourself can be very stressful. Thunder thinking with your friends or colleagues can help you get more done in less time - with a better quality of results. It can also be more fun and mutually profitable.

Play to keep your creativity alive. Spend time playing with children - yours, or borrowed ones. Being with 'childlike' people is a good way to access the playful part of yourself. This spontaneous part of 'you' is very important to the creative process.

Being willing to explore with childlike abandon and adventure is the secret to the creative process. Give children a set of blocks and they create whole worlds without concern for what we might think; cities, forts, houses, castles, boats, etc. Their imagination will amaze you.

Information, time, and the ability to solve problems creatively are the most valued currencies in business today.

We are learning to use technology (Internet, tablets, and smart phones) to access information quickly. How do we learn to access creative thinking?

Attend a seminar (like one of ours); listen to a tape, read a book, buy some of the new creative thinking software like Idea-Fisher, and play. Any one of these will help you raise your Creative IQ and help protect and increase your business and career. Invest in your future; after all, it is where you will spend the rest of your life!

Laugh a lot and have fun. Recently I read that we've lost the sense of laughter. Evidently we now only laugh 6 minutes per day on average compared to 18 minutes per day average just 25 years ago. Humor is a good form of relaxation and brain stimulation. While in this frame of mind we generate more ideas and better ideas.

Use 'fun stuff' in group sessions to facilitate creativity and laugher, e.g. crayons for note taking, candy, funny prizes for silly and bizarre ideas. Have fun and generate more ideas.

Play the 'what if?' game to jump-start your creativity. Change your perspective or basis of looking at the idea or problem at hand. Ask yourself…. What can I add? Shrink? Expand? Take away? Adapt? Modify? Substitute? Reverse? Put to another use? You might just be pleasantly surprised at the answers to your questions. See page 26 for more ideas.

Being wrong is part of the creative process. Creativity in problem solving will lead you down many paths, some of which are dead ends. But being wrong is only a part of the process until you reach a solution. You only have to be right once and that's the one that counts. The wrongs and dead ends are only stepping-stones to your eventual success.

Stressed out - not feeling creative? **Take a fun break and visit a toy store.** Play with the toys or at least watch the children doing so. It will help the stress melt away and it might make the clerks a bit nervous or at least smile.

Get past the fear of looking stupid to the risk of success in accessing and acting on your creativity. Our biggest roadblock to creative thought is often our fear of looking stupid, appearing different, or looking out of place or silly. Most of this goes back to the roots of experience as kids and seeing or experiencing how kids who were different were viewed and treated. Kids who were seen as nerds or weirdoes. But, ask **Bill Gates** if that matters now?

Believe in 'YOU' as a creative source. Many people do not believe they are creative. You may never be a Michael Jordan, a Tom Hanks, or an Elton John - but you can still act and play and enjoy life in those areas. You don't have to be an Einstein or Michelangelo to be a strong creative thinker and generate ideas to act on in your life and business.

Don't let the negative get to you. Remember the majority has historically been wrong. Progress and achievement have come, for the most part, from people who were willing to go their own way, to be wrong in the world's eyes in the pursuit of their dreams. Back in the mid-40's the CEO of 20th Century Fox thought people would soon tire of staring at the box we call TV.

Here are a few additional 'points to ponder' as you work to enhance your creative muscles and innovative mindset.

"Creativity is the natural extension of our enthusiasm." Earl Nightingale

"Creativity involves taking what you have, where you are, and getting the most out of it." Carl Mays

"Creativity is like a muscle - it has to be stretched and exercised regularly to keep it fit and functioning." Gloria Hoffman and Pauline Graivier

"The creative person is the master rather than the slave of his imagination." Michael LeBoeuf, PhD

"Be brave enough to live creatively. The creative is the place where no one else has ever been. You have to leave the city of your comfort and go into the wilderness of your intuition. You can't get there by bus, only by hard work, risking and by not quite knowing what you're doing. What you'll discover will be wonderful: Yourself!" Alan Alda

"When you get a grip on the fear that is holding you back, you will see your creativity soar." Bob 'Idea Man' Hooey 1996

"Creativity is especially expressed in the ability to make connections, to make associations, to turn things around and express them in a new way." Tim Hansen

"I submit that creativity will never be a science - in fact, much of it will always remain a mystery, as much of a mystery as 'what makes the heart tick?' At the same time, I submit that creative is an art - an applied art, a workable art, a learnable art - an art in which all of us can make ourselves more and more proficient, if we will." Alex Osborn

Tackle your fears to unleash your creativity. Society itself, traditions, and self-imposed limitations can build barriers.

Fears can severely hinder the cultivation of creativity.

* Fear of making mistakes

* Fear of being seen as a fool

* Fear of being alone

* Fear of being misused

* Fear of losing the love of the group

* Fear of losing the security of habit

* Fear of being criticized

* Fear of being an individual

* Fear of disturbing tradition or going against prevailing thought.

Don't let your fears stop you from creating the future you want! Feel the fear and do it anyway is a great reminder to move ahead and creatively move through the obstacles in your way.

"The evidence is overwhelming: people, not machines, are the driving force behind our new economic realities. The principle organizations must follow today is the creative use of workers' full abilities, as they purposefully develop strategies to ratchet up the brainpower within the corporate vault." Grace McGartland, 'Thunderbolt Thinking'

113

Challenge your mind – apply mind teasers

Mind teasers are a great way to warm up your creativity.

Take a few of these and play with them. I find using one of two of these or a brain booster to be a great way to warm up my mind and to engage my creative muscles. Athletes, singers, and musicians understand the wisdom of warming up before exercising or performing. **Top performing leaders, professionals, and business people have learned the value of being mentally prepared to engage and win in their arena.** *Note: People send me things like this all the time. Enjoy! If you have some you'd like to add to the list, send them along: bob@ideaman.net*

Here are some good quotes/mind teasers to fuel your creativity

1. Save the whales. Collect the whole set.
2. A day without sunshine is like, night.
3. On the other hand… you have different fingers.
4. I just got lost in thought. It was unfamiliar territory.
5. 42.7 percent of all statistics are made up on the spot.
6. 99 percent of lawyers give the rest a bad name… or do they?
7. I feel like I'm diagonally parked in a parallel universe.
8. You have the right to remain silent. Anything you say will be misquoted and then used against you.
9. I wonder how much deeper the ocean would be without sponges.
10. Honk if you love peace and quiet.
11. Remember half the people you know are below average.
12. Despite the cost of living, have you noticed how popular it remains?
13. Nothing is foolproof to a talented fool.
14. Atheism is a non-prophet organization.
15. He who laughs last thinks slowest.
16. Depression is merely anger without enthusiasm.
17. Eagles may soar, but weasels don't get sucked into jet engines.
18. The early bird may get the worm, but the second mouse gets the cheese.
19. I drive way too fast to worry about cholesterol.
20. I intend to live forever - so far so good.
21. Borrow money from a pessimist - they don't expect it back.
22. If Barbie is so popular, why do you have to buy her friends?

23. My mind is like a steel trap - rusty and illegal in 37 states and provinces.

24. Quantum mechanics: The dreams stuff is made of.

25. The only substitute for good manners is fast reflexes and fast feet.

26. Support bacteria - they're the only culture some people have.

27. When everything's coming your way, you're in the wrong lane and going the wrong way.

28. If at first you don't succeed, destroy all evidence that you tried.

29. A conclusion is the place where you got tired of thinking.

30. Experience is something you don't get until just after you need it.

31. For every action there is an equal and opposite criticism.

32. Bills travel through the mail at twice the speed of checks.

33. Never do card tricks for the group you play poker with.

34. No one is listening until you make a mistake.

35. Success always occurs in private and failure in full view.

36. The colder the x-ray table the more of your body is required on it

37. The hardness of butter is directly proportional to the softness of the bread.

38. The severity of the itch is inversely proportional to the ability to reach it.

39. To steal ideas from one person is plagiarism; to steal from many is research.

40. To succeed in politics, it is often necessary to rise above your principles.

41. Monday is an awful way to spend 1/7th of your life.

42. You never really learn to swear until you learn to drive.

43. Two wrongs are only the beginning.

44. The problem with the gene pool is that there is no lifeguard.

45. The sooner you fall behind the more time you'll have to catch up.

46. A clear conscience is usually the sign of a bad memory.

47. Change is inevitable except from vending machines.

48. Get a new car for your spouse - it'll be a great trade!

49. Plan to be spontaneous - tomorrow.

50. Always try to be modest and be proud of it!

51. If you think nobody cares, try missing a couple of payments.

52. How many of you believe in telekinesis? Raise my hand...

53. Love may be blind but marriage is a real eye-opener.

54. If at first you don't succeed, then skydiving isn't for you.

Can you think of others? Similar to our Brain Boosters, allow your mind to 'play' with the way you look at life and the creative, interesting, thought provoking things that make it up.

Synergy revived

Synergy has a number of applications in our lives, our careers, and our businesses

Synergy as a driver or operating efficiencies: revisiting the re-engineering concept to see what changes can still be made to assist in making your processes more effective or streamlined.

Synergy in marketing: for example the use of cross platform campaigns by media companies to explore their motion picture, publishing, and merchandising properties. Disney and The Lion King used this strategy to go from $50 million to $3 Billion in total revenues.

Synergy as a transformational strategy for business.

For example:

- MTV – a blending of cable TV and pre-recorded music
- Computer video games – descended from earlier board games, arcade games, and PC connections. Thousands of new Apps to download.
- Netflix – replaced the local video store. Blogs replacing tradition media.
- TiVo – video on demand (private TV station) Also, think **YouTube**!
- **Roy Speer** and **Lowell Paxson** noticed people liked shopping and watching TV. The Home Shopping Network, a 24 hour shopping channel was launched.
- Internet shopping – **Amazon** – you can shop and ship around the world.

Synergy works because it mirrors how we now live. How are you equipped to use it?

- Multi-tasking
- Parallel processing
- Multiple channels

"You can't just take a stodgy organization, hire smart guys, and expect good things to happen."

Julio Rotemberg, Fortune Magazine

Found this adv many years ago in an old copy of The Saturday Evening Post. It still hangs on my wall by my 'Think Tank' (downstairs hot tub) as an inspiration to continue my creative leadership and to take risks in my life.

117

I dare you!

Remember growing up and being dared to do something? Remember how often you actually accomplished it, in spite of your own self doubts and fears? Well, I want to share a big DARE. But first, let me tell you the quick story of a young man named **Bill**, who responded to a personal DARE and changed his life, his world, and perhaps ours as well.

Bill was not a healthy boy; in fact you might even have called him 'sickly'. His family moved from the country to the city where he encountered a teacher who was serious about health. As he wrote later, *"It was like he had singled me out."* His teacher, George Krall challenged him one day. He looked straight at Bill and said, *"I dare you to be the healthiest boy in class!"*

Young Bill responded and soon built a body that equaled and outlasted the strongest boys in his class. In fact, he never lost a day at work because of illness and lived a healthy and productive life. He served honorably during the 1st World War and returned to lead his fledgling company to greater success and profit during the great depression. He passed away in 1955, at 85, when the average life expectancy was a good 20 years lower, in part because he had responded to that dare.

Bill launched a company which grew to be one of North America's largest corporations, providing employment for thousands of people. People who were challenged or dared by their president and later Chairman of the Board to push themselves to be strong, **to be creative**, to take risks, to build character, and to share with others. For nearly 40 years, Bill wrote a weekly inspirational "Monday *Morning Message*" for his employees, colleagues and associates.

In a 1955 Monday Morning Message, when he was 84, he pointed out the personal significance of some of these unchanging fundamentals. *"Some folks are continually making changes,"* he said. *"I flatter myself that I like new ventures and new experiences. But when it comes to fundamentals, I believe in finding the right foundations and building on them. I'm a poor changer. For instance, here are some of the fundamentals I have never changed: I have been a church member for over 60 years; married to one wife for over 60 years; a lodge member for over 60 years; and a Purina man for over 60 years."*

Young Bill in this story is, of course, **William H. Danforth**, founder of the Ralston Purina Company, founder of the American Youth Foundation Camps, and author of 14 books including, **I Dare You!**

The copy I bought in 1976 was in its 26th printing. Bill Danforth's life and his writings have challenged hundreds of thousands (*including me*) to live life as an adventure and to stretch and grow in our careers and in our service to others.

I want to leave you with the following personal challenge:

I Dare You:

- To believe in yourself, your experience, your creativity, and your skills.
- To push yourself to learn and hone your skills for greater success.
- To take at least one course every quarter to enhance your skills.
- To take increased responsibility and personal leadership in your role.
- To tap into your creativity and allow innovation to flow.
- To support and encourage your fellow team members to grow.
- To never allow anyone or anything to stop you from succeeding in your role and in life.

Finally I dare you to be the example for others by creatively living life as an adventure and pushing past your comfort zone into the winner's zone.

Innovative ideas in retail

Looking for ways to make your client's shopping experience more 'enjoyable' is worthy of your investment. Here are some savvy retailers who created innovative ideas to help their clients have more fun while shopping. Gee, what a novel idea!

For example, technology company, **Hointer** added QR codes/tags to jeans in their test store so that customers (mainly focused on helping men) could scan the code and get their size delivered to a changing room ready for them try on. This streamlined process saves them time in not having to dig through piles of jeans. Love this concept – trust it will roll out wider.

China based on-line grocer, **Yihodian** has developed augmented reality stores accessed in selective public locations. Clients simply point their smartphone at locations such as public squares where a virtual store is displayed. Items appear to sit on shelves or visually hang from the walls.

NY based furniture retailer, **COCO-MAT** offers a try-before-you-buy approach for their beds. Visitors are allowed to nap in the beds for an hour or two. Following their nap, they receive a free glass of orange juice, but are not obliged to buy after trying.

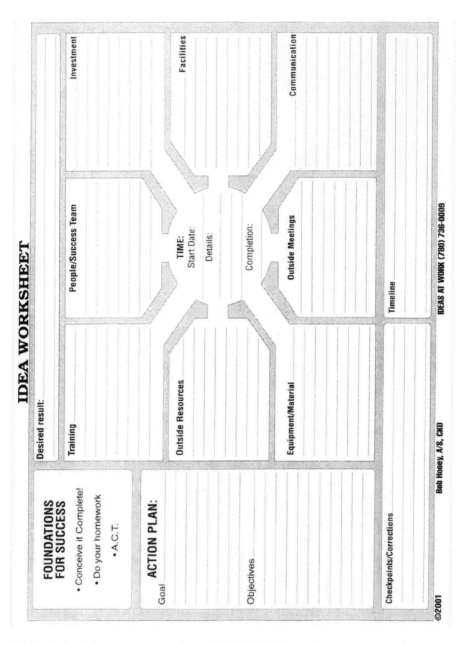

We've included a spare copy of my IDEA Worksheet for your personal use. Visit **www.SuccessPublications.ca/Think.htm** to download larger copies for your personal use.

Bob's B.E.S.T. publications

Bob is a prolific author who has been capturing and sharing his wisdom and experience in print and electronic formats for the past fifteen plus years. In addition to the following publications, several of them best sellers; he has written for consumer, corporate, professional associations, trade, and on-line publications. He has been engaged to write and assist on publications by other best-selling writers and successful companies. His publications are listed to give you an idea of the scope and topics he writes about. Bob's **B**usiness **E**nhancement **S**uccess **T**ools.

Leadership, business, and career development series

- **Running TOO Fast?** (7th edition updated 2014)
- **Legacy of Leadership** (2nd Edition updated 2013)
- **Make ME Feel Special!** The Art of Customer Service (5th Edition)
- **Why Didn't I THINK of That?** (6th Edition – updated 2014)
- **Speaking for Success!** (7th Edition updated 2012)
- A Quest for Balance (SFS companion)
- **Creating TIME to Sell, Lead, or Manage** (2nd Edition 2012)
- Think Beyond the FIRST Sale (2nd Edition 2012)
- Create the Future!
- CONFLICT - Dealing effectively with conflict
- Get to YES! - The subtle art of persuasion in negotiation (EPUB 2011)
- For Immediate Release – The Personal Power of Public Relations
- Media Management - What to say if a reporter calls
- Winning in the Boardroom – Maximized meetings that get results
- THINK Before You Ink! (EPUB 2011)
- Running to Win! (EPUB 2011)
- Coaching for Optimal Results
- Success Skills for leaders, entrepreneurs, and those who support them

Bob's Mini-book series

- TALK, So People Will Listen
- The Courage to Lead!
- LEAD, So People Will Follow
- Creativity Counts!
- Generate More Sales (2nd Edition EPUB 2014)
- Success - Sampler and Companion
- Unleash your Business Potential
- My 'Next' Million Dollar Idea Book
- Learn to Listen
- Thanks Mom!
- Dad, You're Still My Hero!

Bob's Pocket Wisdom series

- Pocket Wisdom for Selling Professionals
- Pocket Wisdom for Speakers
- Pocket Wisdom for Innovators
- Pocket Wisdom for Leaders – Power of One!
- Pocket Wisdom for Business Builders
- Additional PW books are coming in 2014

Co-authored e-books created by Bob
- Quantum Success – 3 volume series
- **In The Company of Leaders** (2nd Edition 2014)
- **Foundational Success** (2nd Edition 2013)

Visit: www.SuccessPublications.ca for more information on Bob's publications and other success resources.

Want to empower your team? Ask about our volume discount packages for *'Why Didn't I THINK of That?'* **Write us at: bob@ideaman.net**

"Innovation is a learned skill of observation and application – Ideas At Work!"

Bob 'Idea Man' Hooey
'My 'NEXT' Million Dollar Idea Book'

Thanks for purchasing and reading
'Why Didn't I THINK of That?'

Each time I prepare to step on the stage; each time I sit down to write or in this case to re-write, I am challenged to deliver something that will be of use-it-now value to my audience/reader.

- I ask myself, *"If I was reading this, what value would I be looking for?"*
- As well as, *"Why is this relevant to me, today?"*

These two questions help to keep me focused and clear on my objectives. They help to remind me to dig into my experiences, stories, examples, and research to provide solid information that will be of benefit and help our readers, when they apply it, succeed. That can be an exciting challenge!

I trust we have done that for you in this updated primer on creating enhanced business success. **'*Why Didn't I THINK of That? The creative power of Ideas At Work*'** is my attempt to capture some of the lessons learned first-hand from observing and working with some tremendously creative leaders, retailers, service providers, and business owners.

Bob 'Idea Man' Hooey
2011 Spirit of CAPS recipient
www.ideaman.net
www.HaveMouthWillTravel.com

Connect with me on:

- **Facebook:** www.facebook.com/bob.hooey
- **LinkedIn:** www.linkedin.com/in/canadianideamanbobhooey
- **YouTube:** www.youtube.com/ideamanbob
- **Smashwords:** www.smashwords.com/profile/view/Hooey
- **Follow me on Twitter:** @IdeamanHooey
- **Snail mail:** Box 10, Egremont, Alberta, T0A0Z0, CANADA

Richard Barton, who launched Zillow, Expedia, Glassdoor, and others says he benefits from repeatedly asking himself a simple question: *"What piece of marketplace information do people crave and don't have?"*

About the author

Bob 'Idea Man' Hooey is a charismatic, confident leader, corporate trainer, inspiring facilitator, Emcee, prolific author, and award winning motivational keynote speaker on leadership, creativity, success, business innovation, and enhancing team performance.

Using personal stories drawn from rich experience, he challenges his audiences to engage his **Ideas At Work!** – To act on what they hear, with clear, innovative building-blocks and field-proven success techniques to increase their effectiveness. Bob challenges them to hone specific 'success skills' critical to their personal and professional advancement.

Bob outlines real-life, results-based, innovative ideas personally drawn from 29 plus years of rich leadership experience in retail, construction, small business, entrepreneurship, manufacturing, association, consulting, community service, sales, and commercial management.

Bob's conversational, often humorous, professional, and sometimes provocative style continues to inspire and challenge his audiences across North America. Bob's motivational, innovative, challenging, and practical **Ideas At Work!** have been successfully applied by thousands of leaders and professionals across the globe. Busy man – productive man!

Bob is a frequent contributor to North American consumer, corporate, association, trade, and on-line publications on leadership, success, employee motivation and training; as well as creativity and innovative problem solving, priority and time management, and effective customer service. He is the inspirational author of 30 plus publications, including several best-selling print, e-books, reader style e-pubs, and a Pocket Wisdom series.

Visit: **www.SuccessPublications.ca** for more information.

Retired, award winning kitchen designer, Bob Hooey, CKD-Emeritus was one of only 75 Canadian designers to earn this prestigious certification by the US based National Kitchen and Bath Association.

In December 2000, Bob was given a special CAPS National Presidential award **"…for his energetic contribution to the advancement of CAPS and his living example of the power of one"** in addition to being elected to the CAPS National Board. He has been recognized by the National Speakers Association and other groups for his leadership contributions.

Bob is a co-founder and a Past President of the CAPS Vancouver Chapter and served as 2012 President of the CAPS Edmonton Chapter. He is a member of the NSA-Arizona Chapter and an active leader in the National Speakers Association, a charter member of the Canadian Association of Professional Speakers, as well as the Global Speakers Federation. He has just retired (December 2013) as a Trustee (after 5 years) from the CAPS Foundation.

In 1998, Toastmasters International recognized Bob **"…for his professionalism and outstanding achievements in public speaking"**. That August in Palm Desert, California Bob became the 48th speaker in the world to be awarded this prestigious professional level honor as an **Accredited Speaker**. He has been inducted into their Hall of Fame on numerous occasions for his leadership contributions.

Bob has been honoured by the United Nations Association of BC (1993) and received the **CANADA 125 award** (1992) for his ongoing leadership contributions to the community. In 1998, Bob joined 3 other men to sail a 65 foot gaff rigged schooner from Honolulu, Hawaii to Kobe, Japan, barely surviving a 'baby' typhoon enroute.

In November 2011 Bob was awarded the Spirit of CAPS at their annual convention, becoming the 11th speaker to earn this prestigious CAPS National award. Visit: **www.ideaman.net/SoC.htm**

Bob loves to travel and his speaking and writing have allowed him to visit 44 countries so far. Perhaps your organization would like to bring Bob in to share a few ideas with your leaders and teams around the globe.

Visit: **www.HaveMouthWillTravel.com** for more information.

Acknowledgements, credits, and disclaimers

As with each of my books, a very special dedication to the two people who meant the most to me, my folks **Ron and Marge Hooey**. Sadly, both my parents left this earthly realm in 1999. I still miss our time together and your encouragement and love. I was blessed with the two of you in my life.

תודה
Dankie Gracias شكراً
Спасибо Merci Takk
Köszönjük Terima kasih
Grazie Dziękujemy Děkojame
Ďakujeme Vielen Dank Paldies
Kiitos Täname teid 謝謝
Tak
感謝您 Obrigado Teşekkür Ederiz
Σας Ευχαριστούμ 감사합니다
ขอบคุณ
Bedankt Děkujeme vám
ありがとうございます
Tack

Thank You

To my inspiring wife and professional proof reader and publications coach, **Irene Gaudet**, who loves, encourages, and supports me in my quest to continue sharing my **Ideas At Work!** across the world. Thank you seems so inadequate for your timely work in helping make my writing and my client service better! I love the time we spend together! A special dedication to Irene's dad, **George Sidor**, who left us April 7th, 2014. George was a wonderful man who created a spot in his heart for me.

My thanks to the many people who have encouraged me in my growth as a leader, speaker, and engaging trainer in each area of expertise including *'Why Didn't I THINK of That?'* Perhaps you'll understand why they call me the 'Idea Man'.

- To my colleagues and friends in the National Speakers Association **(NSA)**, the Canadian Association of Professional Speakers **(CAPS)**, and the Global Speakers Federation **(GSF)** who continually challenge me to strive for success and increased excellence. To **Nabil Doss** who inspires me.

- To my many friends and family around the world, to whom I owe an un-payable debt of gratitude for your investment, encouragement, time, and support when I was just starting down this path; and oh, so rough around the edges. To those who shared stories included here.

- **To my great audiences, leaders, students, coaching clients, and readers across the globe** who share their experiences and enjoyment of my work. Your positive and supportive feedback encourages me to keep working on additional programs and success publications like this updated version. My experience with you creates the foundation for additional real-life experiences I can take from the stage to the page, the classroom to the boardroom.

- My thanks to a 'select' few friends for your ongoing support and 'constructive' abuse. You know who you are.

Disclaimer

We have not attempted to cite all the authorities and sources consulted in the preparation of this book. To do so would require much more space than is available. The list would include departments of various governments, libraries, industrial institutions, periodicals, and many individuals. Inspiration was drawn from many sources, including other books by the author, in this updated creation of *'Why Didn't I THINK of That?'*

This book is written and designed to provide information on more effective use of your time in attracting and retaining clients, and as a life and leadership enhancement guide. It is sold with the 'explicit' understanding that the publisher and/or the author(s) are **not** engaged in rendering legal, accounting, or other professional services. If legal or other expert assistance is required, the services of a competent professional in your geographic area should be sought.

It is not the purpose of this book to reprint all the information that is otherwise available. Its primary purpose is to complement, amplify, and supplement other books and reference materials already available. You are encouraged to search out and study all the available material, learn as much as possible, and tailor the information to your individual needs. This will help to enhance your success in being a more effective leader or professional.

Every effort has been made to make this book as complete and as accurate as possible within the scope of its focus. However, there may be mistakes, both typographical and in content or attribution. Care has been taken to trace ownership of copyright material contained in this volume. The publisher will gladly receive information that will allow him to rectify any reference or credit line in subsequent editions. This book should be used only as a general guide and not as the ultimate source of information. Furthermore, this book contains information that is current only up to the date of publication.

The purpose of *'Why Didn't I THINK of That?'* is to educate and entertain; perhaps to inform and to inspire. It is certainly to challenge its readers to learn and apply its secrets and tips, to challenge them to enhance their skills and leverage their time to create more productive outcomes within their respective businesses in better serving their clients and customers.

The author and publisher shall have **neither** liability **nor** responsibility to any person or entity with respect to any loss or damage caused, or alleged to have been caused, directly or indirectly, by the information contained in this book.

What they say about Bob 'Idea Man' Hooey

As I travel across North America, and more recently around the globe, sharing my **Ideas At Work!** I am fortunate to get feedback and comments from my audiences and colleagues. These comments come from people who have been touched, challenged, or simply enjoyed themselves in one of my sessions. **I'd love to come and share some ideas with your organization and teams.**

"I've known Bob for several years and follow his activities in business with interest. I originally met Bob when he spoke for a Rotary Leadership Institute and got to know him better when he came to Vladivostok, Russia to speak to our leadership. **When you spoke I thought you were one of us because you talked about our challenges just like yours.** *You could understand the others, which makes you a great speaker!"* **Andrey Konyushok,** *Rotary International District 2225 Governor 2012-2013, far eastern Russia*

"I still get comments from people about your presentation. **Only a few speakers have left an impression that lasts that long.** *You hit a spot with the tourism people."* **Janet Bell,** *Yukon Economic Forums*

"We greatly appreciate **the energy and effort you put into researching and adapting your keynote to make it more meaningful to our member councils.** *Early feedback from our delegates indicates that this year's convention was one of our most successful events yet, and we thank you for your contribution to this success."* **Larry Goodhope,** *Executive Director Alberta Association of Municipal Districts and Counties*

"Thank you Bob; it is **always a pleasure to see a true professional at work.** *You have made the name 'Speaker' stand out as a truism - someone who encourages people to examine their lives and make adjustments. The personal stories you shared with your audience made such a great impression on everyone.* **The comments indicated you hit people right where it is important - in their hearts.** *Each of those in your audience took away a new feeling of personal success and encouragement."* **Sherry Knight,** *Dimension Eleven Human Resources and Communications*

"Bob is one of those rare individuals who knows how to tackle obstacles in life to reach his dreams. He takes each as a **learning experience and stretches for more.** *His compassion and genuine interest in others, make him an exceptional coach."* **Cindy Kindret,** *Training Manager, Silk FM Radio*

*"Without doubt, **I have gained immeasurable self-assurance.** Bob, your patience and your encouragement has been much appreciated. **I strongly recommend your course to anyone looking for self-improvement and professional development.**"* **Jeannie Mura**, *Human Resources Chevron Canada*

*"I am pleased to recommend Bob 'Idea Man' Hooey to any organization looking for a charismatic, confident speaker and seminar leader. I have seen Bob in action on several occasions, and he is ALWAYS on! Bob has the ability to grab his audience's attention and keep it. Quite simply, **if Bob is involved - your program or seminar is guaranteed to succeed.**"* **Maurice Laving**, *Coordinator Training and Development, London Drugs*

*"I have found **Bob's attention to detail** and his ability to fine tune his seminars to match the time frame and needs of the audience to be a valuable asset to our educational program."* **Patsy Schell**, *Executive Director Surrey Chamber of Commerce*

*"Great seeing you in Cancun and congratulations on a job well done. **The seminar was a great success! Your humorous and conversational style was a tremendous asset.** It is my sincere hope that we can be associated again at future seminars."* **Donald MacPherson**, *Attorney At Law, Phoenix, Arizona*

*"**What a great conference.** It was a great pleasure meeting with you at the Ritz Carlton, Cancun and I shall look forward to hopefully welcoming you and your family in Dublin, Ireland someday."* **A. Paul Ryan**, *Petronva Corporation, Dublin, Ireland*

*"Congratulations on the **Spirit of CAPS Award.** You have worked long and hard on behalf of CAPS ...**helped many speakers including me** and richly deserve this award. Well done my friend."* **Peter Legge**, *CSP, Hof, CPAE*

*"I had the pleasure of hearing and watching Bob Hooey deliver a keynote speech several years ago when he gave a presentation at a Toastmasters International Convention. **Bob impressed me greatly with his professionalism, energy, and ability to connect with his audience while giving them value.** I heartily recommend this talented speaker and 'Idea Man' to all who want to move to the next level."* **Dr. Dilip Abayasekara**, *DTM, Accredited Speaker, Past President, Toastmasters International*

*"I attended **Speaking for Success** in Edmonton. **The mark of a true leader is someone who will lay down their own pride to teach all they know to their potential successors.** To be taught by a man of his caliber was an honor whether you're a beginner like myself or a professional; the experience is well worth it! To Bob - it truly was an honor to meet you. Stay humble and enjoy the great success."*
Samantha McLeod

Engage Canada's 'Idea Man' for your leaders and their teams

"I have been so excited working with Bob Hooey, as he has given inspiration and motivation to our leadership team members. Both at the Brick Warehouse – Alberta and here at Art Van Furniture – Michigan; with his years of experience in working with business executives and his humorous and delightful packaging of his material, he makes learning with Bob a real joy. But most importantly, anyone who comes in contact with his material is the better for it." **Kim Yost**, CEO Art Van Furniture, former CEO The Brick

Motivate your teams, your employees, and your leaders to 'productively' grow, enhance their creative muscles, and 'profitably' succeed!

- Protect your conference investment - leverage your training dollars.
- Enhance your professional career and sell more products and services.
- Equip and motivate your leaders and their teams to grow and succeed, 'even' in tough times!
- Leverage your time to enhance your skills, equip your teams, and better serve your clients.
- Leverage your leadership and investment of time to leave a significant legacy within your organization and life!

Call today to engage best-selling author, award winning, inspirational leadership keynote speaker, leaders success coach, and employee development trainer, **Bob 'Idea Man' Hooey** and his innovative, audience based, results-focused, **Ideas At Work!** for your next company, convention, leadership, staff, training, or association event. You'll be glad you did!

Call 1-780-736-0009 to connect with Bob 'Idea Man' Hooey today!
Learn more about Bob at: www.ideaman.net

"On very short notice Bob cleared his schedule and graciously presented at our meeting when the original speaker was unable to attend. **Bob set the tone for our two-day leadership meeting and gave us all a motivational lift.** *His compassion and true interest in people was clearly evident, making him very credible. He shared some great stories, has a wealth of experience and knowledge, and it was a pleasure listening to him. His down-to-Earth style makes it easier to retain the information presented. He also followed up with additional info and handouts, cementing his message of building bridges, not walls. Fantastic job, Bob, and thanks again!"* **Barbara Afra Beler**, MBA, Senior Specialist Commercial Community, Alberta North, **BMO Bank of Montreal**

73194931R00072

Made in the USA
Columbia, SC
07 September 2019